The Essence of Wiccan Living and Lifestyle

Crafting a Magical Life: Exploring the Wiccan Living and Lifestyle

Olivia Turner

Table of Contents

INTRODUCTION

Welcome to "The Essence of Wiccan Living and Lifestyle: Crafting a Magical Life." This book is your guide to exploring and embracing the rich, mystical world of Wicca. Whether new to the path or seeking to deepen your practice, this journey will offer insights into the ancient traditions and modern practices that define Wiccan living.

Wicca is more than a religion; it is a way of life that harmonizes with the cycles of nature and the earth's rhythms. Rooted in pre-Christian pagan traditions, Wicca was revitalized in the mid-20th century and blossomed into a diverse and vibrant spiritual path. This book delves into its historical roots, core beliefs, and the ethical framework that guides Wiccans today.

Throughout these pages, you will be captivated by the beauty and wonder of the Wiccan Wheel of the Year, the sacred Sabbats that mark the changing seasons, and the deep reverence for the divine in its many forms. This exploration will inspire you with the deities worshipped, the tools and symbols used in rituals, and the magickal practices that form the heart of Wiccan spirituality.

By the end of this book, you will have a profound understanding of how to practically integrate Wiccan principles into your daily life, crafting a magical existence filled with purpose, balance, and harmony. This knowledge will empower you to set off on this fascinating voyage to discover the spirit of Wicca and its way of life.

CHAPTER I

Get To Know Wicca

Understanding Wicca

Wicca is a contemporary witchcraft and pagan religion whose rituals and theological framework are based on various hermetic and old pagan and 20th-century themes. Wicca has a complicated history that blends parts of contemporary religious movements with folklore from antiquity and the Middle Ages. Gerald Gardner, a retired British civil servant who claimed to have been admitted into a coven of witches in the New Forest, England, first brought it to the public's attention in the early 20th century. The publications "Witchcraft Today" and "The Meaning of Witchcraft," in particular, by Gardner, set the groundwork for the practices and writings that would eventually be called Wicca. His assertion that Wicca was the surviving form of an old-fashioned, pre-Christian religion has generated much discussion and disagreement among academics.

Wicca is a duotheistic religion that honors a God and a Goddess, frequently understood to symbolize the masculine and feminine facets of nature and divinity. These gods are often connected to the Triple Goddess, who represents the phases of a woman's existence, including maiden, mother, and crone, and the Horned God, who stands for the untamed, masculine elements of nature. The Triple Goddess is connected to figures like the Greek Hecate or the Roman Diana, while the Horned God is frequently connected to historical deities like the Celtic Cernunnos. Wicca celebrates life, death, and rebirth cycles via rites and practices centered on the moon's phases and the varying seasons.

Wicca also embraces the idea of magic, which is understood as an innate force that may be used by performing rituals and casting spells. This magic is frequently used for self-actualization, healing, and protection. Witches who practice Wicca use cauldrons, athames (ritual knives), and wands in their rituals. Wicca is a very individualized practice, with many covens and traditions creating distinctive rituals and interpretations of the basic principles.

One of the most widespread myths regarding Wicca is that it is the same as Satanism. This misconception most likely originates from centuries of Christian persecution of heathen customs and the conflating of witchcraft with idolatry of the devil. But Wiccans reject the existence of Satan and all other figures that resemble the Christian devil. Instead, they see their gods as representations of nature, emphasizing balance, harmony, and respect for all living things. Wicca is a nature-based religion emphasizing the interdependence of all life and ecological consciousness.

Another widespread misperception is that Wiccans perform evil deeds or cast spells. In actuality, most Wiccans follow the Wiccan Rede, a fundamental moral precept that reads, "An it harm none, do what ye will." This principle focuses on non-harm and encourages ethical behavior and personal accountability. The Threefold Law, which maintains that any energy a person releases into the universe—positive or negative—will return to them threefold, is another belief held by many Wiccans. This conviction inspires practitioners to behave honorably and kindly.

Another myth is that Wicca is a wholly matriarchal faith that doesn't accept men. Wicca acknowledges and honors both the male and feminine deities, even though it strongly emphasizes the former. Men and women can occupy leadership roles in many mixed-gender Wiccan covens. Wicca's focus on the Goddess balances the patriarchal systems that have ruled many conventional faiths, but it does not lessen the significance of God.

Moreover, some people think that Wicca is an ancient, static religion that has been around for centuries in its current form. Although Wicca has its roots in prehistoric paganism, it is essentially a modern practice. To establish a new religious movement, Gerald Gardner and other early Wiccans combined elements of ceremonial magic, Eastern philosophy, and folklore. Wiccans constantly create new rituals, beliefs, and practices to suit the times, and their traditions continually evolve.

The resurgence of Wicca in the contemporary era began in the middle of the 20th century, at the same time when interest in feminism, environmentalism, and alternative spiritualities started to develop. Gerald Gardner's 1950s public admission of practicing witchcraft ignited a resurgence of interest in paganism and the occult. The works of Gardner and other early Wiccans laid the groundwork for forming a cohesive religious movement. Wicca started to gain popularity outside of the United Kingdom by the 1960s and 1970s, especially in the United States, where it was well-received by people who were fed up with traditional religious organizations.

The 1960s countercultural movements were primarily responsible for Wicca's rise to popularity. Wicca's ideals of individual spiritual empowerment and connection to nature resonated with the era's emphasis on personal independence, awareness inquiry, and rejection of conventional authority. Wicca's popularity was further aided by its affiliation with feminist principles. Wicca's Goddess-centric approach provided a spiritual framework that acknowledged female experience and strength, which was especially appealing as the women's liberation movement grew.

Influential works like "Witchcraft for Tomorrow" by Doreen Valiente and "Buckland's Complete Book of Witchcraft" by Raymond Buckland were published, which helped spread Wiccan beliefs and practices. These books provide easily understood instructions for lone practitioners and those unable to join formal covens, which aided in disseminating Wicca throughout many socioeconomic groups and geographical areas. This process was expedited by the development of the Internet in the latter half of the 20th century, which allowed Wiccans to communicate, exchange knowledge, and form communities virtually.

Due to its famous cultural depiction, Wicca saw increased recognition and acceptability in the 1990s and 2000s. A more favorable and realistic portrayal of witchcraft was presented in television series like "Buffy the Vampire Slayer" and "Charmed," as well as films like "The Craft," which piqued the attention and curiosity of younger audiences. Even though these depictions were frequently exaggerated and incomplete, they helped de-stigmatize witchcraft and raise awareness of Wicca as a respectable spiritual path.

Wicca is a vibrant, diversified religion with adherents worldwide today. It includes a broad variety of traditions, ranging from more eclectic versions that borrow aspects from other spiritual systems to more traditional Wicca, such as Gardnerian and Alexandrian Wicca, which follow the rites and teachings of their founders faithfully. This diversity illustrates how Wicca is naturally adaptable and flexible, appealing to people with various personal and cultural backgrounds.

Wiccans nowadays still place a high value on nature, spiritual development, and moral behavior. Many Wiccans actively participate in social justice and environmental movements because they find a connection between their spiritual practices and their duties to the planet and all people. With many websites, forums, and social media groups devoted to Wiccan subjects, the Internet is invaluable for fostering community and educating people.

Even with increasing acceptance, there are still obstacles and misconceptions surrounding Wicca. Prejudice and discrimination against Wiccans may exist in some parts of the world as a result of persistent prejudices and false beliefs regarding witchcraft. Nonetheless, the growing awareness of Wicca and kindred paganism in popular culture indicates a slow movement toward increased tolerance and comprehension.

To sum up, Wicca is a modern, nature-based religion combining past and present elements to offer a distinctive spiritual path. Numerous individuals looking for an alternative to traditional religious practices find resonance in their emphasis on the harmony of the divine, both masculine and feminine, ethical living, and personal empowerment. Despite enduring myths, Wicca has had a resurgence in the contemporary day and has expanded into a thriving, multifaceted religious movement with a global reach. It is anticipated that increasing knowledge and acceptance of Wicca and other pagan traditions would be attained by ongoing education and discussion, promoting a more accepting and spiritually varied society.

Core Beliefs and Principles

Wicca is a modern pagan religion that emphasizes worshiping the God and the Goddess, practicing witchcraft, and having a deep respect for the natural world. Its fundamental ideas and precepts are diverse, derived from contemporary spiritual activities and many old pagan customs. The basic tenet of Wicca is the interdependence of all life and natural cycles. Wiccans believe that humans are a part of the enormous web of life and that everything in the cosmos is interconnected. Adherents of this ideology are encouraged to live in peace with the environment and are instilled with a strong respect for nature and all living things.

Another essential component of Wicca is the practice of magic, or "magick," as it is sometimes called in Wiccan writings to differentiate it from stage magic. Wicca views magic as utilizing natural forces and energies to bring about change in line with one's will. Wiccans hold that they can positively impact their lives and the world around them through rituals, spells, and working with Earth's energies. Ethical standards govern this discipline, guaranteeing that magic is employed sensibly and without inflicting harm.

One of Wicca's central moral precepts is the Wiccan Rede, which sums up the primary idea of the faith: "An it harm none, do what ye will." This expression strongly emphasizes moral behavior and personal accountability, implying that people are free to follow their dreams and aspirations as long as they don't hurt other people. The Rede encourages Wiccans to think about how their activities affect other people and the environment by promoting a philosophy of non-harm and compassion. It guides practitioners in magical and mundane endeavors, acting as a moral compass.

The thrice Law, which holds that any energy or intent a person sends out into the world—positive or negative—

will return to them significantly, is closely associated with the Wiccan Rede. This belief is similar to karma, which holds that a person's actions have repercussions that affect them personally. In Wicca, the Threefold Law emphasizes the value of moral conduct and individual accountability. Knowing that their acts will directly affect their own life, it urges practitioners to act honorably and kindly. The Threefold Law and the Wiccan Rede together provide the ethical framework for Wicca, encouraging responsible magical practice, self-improvement, and compassion.

Wicca is a monotheistic religion that honors a God and a Goddess as contrasting facets of the divine. The natural powers of the universe are embodied by the God and Goddess, who stand for the concepts of masculinity and femininity. The sun, trees, and wild animals are frequently connected to the God of life, representing vigor, strength, and the life-death cycle. He is commonly shown as the Horned God, a figure with horns or antlers that symbolizes his ties to the natural world and the antiquated pagan gods Pan and Cernunnos.

In contrast, the Goddess is connected to the moon, fertility, and the nurturing elements of the natural world. She is frequently shown as the Triple Goddess, standing for the Maiden, Mother, and Crone phases of a woman's existence. Every facet of the Triple Goddess represents a distinct lunar phase and a range of life events, including the cycles of rebirth, development, and death. The Goddess reflects the sacredness of the Earth and all life, embodying the creative and caring forces of the universe.

Wiccans may acknowledge deities from different pantheons, such as Celtic, Greek, Roman, and Norse traditions, and the God and Goddess. Many view these deities as facets or manifestations of the same divine force. Through a complex and varied spiritual practice, practitioners can connect with the deities that most closely align with their individual experiences and beliefs, thanks to this polytheistic approach.

There is cooperation and mutual respect between Wiccans and their deities. Wiccans frequently perform rituals, prayers, and offerings to respect and converse with the God and Goddess and ask for their direction and blessings. Wicca strongly focuses on living in harmony with the natural world, and these rites are typically carried out by the moon's cycles and the varying seasons.

Wiccan beliefs and practices lay a strong emphasis on nature. Wiccans believe that everything in nature is sacred and contains the divine. This respect for the natural world is demonstrated by customs that honor the moon's cycles (called Esbats) and the seasons (called Sabbats). The eight Sabbats, which include celebrations like Beltane, Yule, and Samhain, commemorate the various stages of the agricultural cycle and indicate significant moments in the Wheel of the Year. These festivals help Wiccans feel more at one with nature by tying them into the planet's cycles.

The primary components of Wiccan cosmology and ritual practice are the elements: Earth, Air, Fire, and Water. Collectively, the elements form a harmonic and well-balanced system, with each component standing for a distinct facet of existence and the natural world. Earth is connected to the tangible world and the earthly parts of existence; it represents fertility, stability, and anchoring. Air is associated with the mind and the breath of life; it symbolizes intelligence, communication, and inspiration. Fire is related to the will and the Spirit and represents passion, transformation, and energy. Water is associated with feelings, intuition, and healing; it also connects to the subconscious and life's flow.

The elements are frequently called upon in Wiccan rituals to establish a sacred area and provide harmony and balance to the event. Usually, a circle is cast to do this, which is a ceremonial act that marks a dedicated area for magical and spiritual work. Practitioners can ask the elements to give their energies within this circle, enhancing and shielding the space for their spells and rituals. The elements are also symbolized on the Wiccan altar by objects like Water in a chalice for Water, Fire for Fire, Air for Air, and Earth for Earth through stones or crystals.

Beyond the practice of rituals, Wicca places great stress on the natural world and the elements. Wiccans consider the preservation and care of the Earth to be a holy duty, and as such, they are frequently very committed to ecology and ecological sustainability. Many Wiccans promote environmental causes through activism, organic farming, and conservation measures. This dedication to the Earth reflects the Wiccan belief in the interdependence of all life and the duty to live in peace with nature.

In Wicca, rituals and symbols are essential for establishing divine connections, commemorating important life events, and using magic to effect desired changes. Wiccan rituals can range from straightforward solitary practices to complex rites involving a coven. These rituals frequently involve particular implements and deeply spiritually significant symbols.

One of the most well-known symbols in Wicca is the pentacle, a five-pointed star enclosed in a circle. The fifth point of the star represents Spirit, the unifying factor that unites all the elements, while the other points represent the elements of Earth, Air, Fire, and Water. The pentacle represents harmony, safety, and the interdependence of all life. It is frequently used in rituals to consecrate and guard the sacred place or worn as a necklace.

The chalice, wand, cauldron, and athame, a ceremonial dagger, are other significant symbols in Wicca. The athame symbolizes the element of Fire and a ritual tool for directing energy. The chalice, which represents the Goddess' womb and is connected to the element of Water, is used to hold ceremonial drinks. The wand is used to summon spirits and deities and to channel energy. It symbolizes the element of Air. The cauldron represents metamorphosis and rebirth and is connected to both the Goddess and the element of Water.

Casting a circle to establish a sacred area is the first step in many Wiccan rituals, which have a predetermined format. The principal ritual or spell is then performed, the circle is closed, and the elements and deities are invoked. These rites can be carried out to commemorate the Sabbats and Esbats, to celebrate significant life events like initiations and handfastings (Wiccan marriages), or to fulfill particular magical objectives.

Wicca is a decentralized, highly individualistic religion that lacks doctrine and a central authority. This makes a lot of variation and individual interpretation possible within the practice. Various Wicca lineages, including Gardnerian, Alexandrian, and Eclectic Wicca, have distinctive rituals, philosophies, and hierarchies. Gerald Gardner founded Gardnerian Wicca, one of the oldest and most traditional versions, emphasizing coven-based practice and initiatory lineage. While there are many parallels between Gardnerian Wicca and Alexandrian Wicca, Alexandrian Wicca was developed by Alex Sanders and includes more ceremonial magic and eclectic components.

The most adaptable and inclusive kind of Wicca is eclectic Wicca, which enables practitioners to construct their unique spiritual pathways by drawing from various sources. Eclectic Wiccans may blend aspects of other paganism, Eastern philosophy, or contemporary spiritual practices into their rites and beliefs. Because of its flexibility, Wicca can be accessed by a broad spectrum of people who can customize their practice to suit their requirements and backgrounds.

The development of Wicca has also been significantly influenced by technology and the internet. Internet discussion boards, Social media pages, and websites devoted to Wiccan subjects have produced online communities where practitioners can celebrate their beliefs, exchange knowledge, and support one another. This has proven especially crucial for lone practitioners and those who reside in places without any tangible Wiccan community. Wicca has become more widely known because of the internet, making it more straightforward for people to learn about and practice the faith.

Wicca continues to encounter difficulties and misunderstandings despite its increased recognition and acceptance. One of the most pervasive myths is the idea that Wicca is the same as devil worship or Satanism. This misconception is the result of popular culture's sensationalized depictions of witches as well as historical links between witchcraft, easy, and devil worship. In actuality, Wiccan beliefs and practices are based on the reverence for nature and the worship of God and Goddess; they do not believe in Satan or any other figure of a similar sort.

The misconception that witches are evil or destructive magic practitioners presents another difficulty. Although Wiccans engage in magic, their practice is governed by moral precepts like the Threefold Law and the Wiccan Rede, which emphasize personal accountability and non-harm. Most Wiccans concentrate on positive, constructive magic intended for protection, healing, and self-improvement. Instead of a realistic representation of Wiccan practice, the image of the evil witch casting curses is primarily a creation of fiction and tradition.

Because of their beliefs, Wiccans may also encounter prejudice or discrimination. Being a witch or Wiccan can result in violence, legal difficulties, and social rejection in some parts of the world. Many Wiccans persevere in practicing their religion publicly despite these obstacles, striving for increased acceptance and comprehension of their beliefs.

To sum up, Wicca is a vast and varied religion that strongly emphasizes worshiping the God and Goddess, practicing ethical magic, and having a deep respect for the natural world. Its fundamental ideals, including the Threefold Law and the Wiccan Rede, encourage compassion, self-reliance, and harmony with the natural world. Wiccan practice is centered on the value of nature and the elements, reflecting a close connection to the Earth's life cycles. Wiccans aim to live in harmony with the natural world and to be in alignment with the divine through rituals, symbols, and the worship of deities. Wicca is a significant spiritual path that offers a connection to nature and the sacred for those who seek it despite obstacles and misconceptions.

The Structure of Wiccan Practice

Wicca is a contemporary pagan and witchcraft religion with various rituals and beliefs centered on reverence for the natural world and celebrating life's cycles. Wiccan practice's flexible and adaptive structure enables practitioners to customize their spiritual journeys to suit their requirements and inclinations. Fundamentally, Wicca emphasizes direct communication with the divine through solo practice or participation in a coven. It is a highly intimate and immersive religion.

The central tenet of Wicca is the worship of the God and Goddess, who are frequently regarded as embodying the natural world. The religion's close ties to nature are reflected in the rites and rituals, which are timed to correspond with the moon's phases and the varying seasons. These practices can range from something as basic as a solitary meditation to something more complex like an elaborate ceremony attended by several practitioners. Whether performed in a group or alone, Wiccan rituals worship the gods, identify critical moments in the solar and lunar cycles, and channel natural energies for magical purposes.

Wicca's practice is characterized by its flexibility, allowing it to be carried out solo or in a coven. Solitary practice is the act of worshiping and performing rituals by oneself without the assistance of an official organization. This method is prevalent among modern Wiccans because it is easy to find materials and information that let people study and practice independently. "Solitaries," or solitary practitioners, are allowed to design their rituals, select their deities, and proceed at their speed on their unique spiritual path.

Practicing alone can be very rewarding since it allows you a great deal of introspection and personal autonomy. Without following a coven's rules, solitaries can modify their methods to suit their schedules and personal convictions. Those who might not have access to a nearby coven prefer a more solitary spiritual path or would like to explore their spirituality free from the dynamics of a group setting can find this practice helpful.

On the other hand, coven-based practice entails gathering Wiccans for ceremonial purposes, Sabbat and Esbat celebrations, and group magical activities. A coven comprises a few practitioners, usually at most thirteen, though this might vary. Coven-based practice provides mutual support, shared learning, and a sense of community. Coven members gain from the group's combined knowledge and experience, and their sense of camaraderie can heighten their spiritual journey.

Coven-based practices frequently take a more structured approach, with hierarchy, initiation rites, and rituals that are set in place. This structure can anchor the practice in a shared history and group experience by establishing a feeling of continuity and tradition. Covens may also provide official instruction and mentorship, enabling newcomers to advance their knowledge and proficiency in Wicca under the direction of seasoned practitioners.

Roles and obligations are usually assigned to coven members to facilitate good group dynamics and efficient ritual performance. Although a coven's hierarchy and organization can differ significantly, certain functions are frequently present in covens of all sizes. Typically, the High Priest and High Priestess serve as the coven's principal leaders, directing rituals, offering spiritual guidance, and supervising the onboarding of new members. In rituals and ceremonies, they embody the divine powers and represent the Goddess and God, respectively.

In many Wiccan traditions, the High Priestess frequently plays a vital role, signifying the significance of the feminine deity. She might assist in organizing the coven's events, guiding newcomers, and acting as the group's spiritual leader. In these responsibilities, the High Priest assists her by providing equilibrium and balancing her leadership with his own.

A coven may also have other responsibilities, such as the Maiden, who supports the High Priestess and helps with ritual preparation; the Summoner or Guard, who guards the circle and oversees the practicalities of meetings; and the Scribe, who maintains minutes of the coven's actions and ceremonies. These positions aid in delegating duties and guarantee that every facet of the coven's operations is covered.

An essential component of the coven-based practice is initiation, which signifies a new member's official admission into the group. While initiation procedures varied throughout Wiccan traditions, they typically entail a time of study and preparation, followed by a rite representing the initiate's dedication to Wicca and the coven. A new magical name, oaths, and purification are everyday symbolic actions associated with this rite of passage.

Wiccans primarily connect with the divine, celebrate nature's cycles, and carry out magical operations through ritual and ceremony, which are central to their practice. These ceremonies have symbolic value and are meant to bring the performer into harmony with the planet's and the universe's natural rhythms. They offer an organized method for paying respect to the Gods and Goddesses, commemorating the passing of time, and using magic to bring about desired transformations.

Casting a circle to establish a sacred area is the first step in many Wiccan rituals, which have a predetermined format. The circle protects and concentrates the practitioners' energy by acting as a wall dividing the ritual's sacred area from the outside world. The elements —Earth, Air, Fire, and Water—are usually called upon within the circle to support the ritual by balancing and harmonizing the area.

The invocation of the God and Goddess, which calls their blessings and presence into the circle, is the main component of many Wiccan ceremonies. Candle lighting or other symbolic objects are frequently used with this invocation, which gestures, chants, or spoken words can carry out. Food, drink, or other objects are offered to the God and Goddess as a sign of appreciation and respect. They are regarded and treasured.

The eight principal points of the Wheel of the Year, which include the solstices, equinoxes, and the midpoints between them, are marked by seasonal rites called Sabbats. These Sabbats honor the natural cycles of planting and harvesting crops, seasonal changes, and the harmony of light and dark. Every Sabbath has distinct themes and meanings corresponding to the particular energies and seasonal changes.

Moon phases, especially the full moon, are honored through lunar rites known as Esbats. The moon is particularly significant in Wicca because it represents the Goddess and the cyclical aspect of existence. Esbats are periods when one can engage in introspection, divination, and magical practices while harnessing the vital energies connected to the lunar cycle.

Wiccan ceremonies can commemorate essential life milestones like births, handfastings (Wiccan marriages), initiations, and seasonal and lunar rituals. These ceremonies mark significant turning points and life changes and are rich with symbolic meaning. An initiation ceremony, for instance, can entail symbolic acts of rebirth and transformation. In contrast, a handfasting ceremony might involve joining hands with a cord to signify the couple's unity.

Wiccan ceremonies heavily incorporate the use of tools and symbols. The chalice, pentacle, wand, and athame (a ceremonial knife) are familiar ritual implements. Every tool represents distinct components and facets of the practice, each with its symbolic meaning and purpose. For example, the chalice represents the feminine divine and stores ritual liquids; the athame casts the circle and directs energy. The pentacle represents all life's elements and unity, frequently engraved with a five-pointed star.

In Wicca, rituals aim to provide the practitioner with a profoundly changing experience in addition to carrying out predetermined activities. They offer a pathway to heightened consciousness, a means of establishing a connection with the divine, and an opportunity for spiritual and personal development. Practitioners can develop a sense of oneness and connection by attuning themselves to the energies of the natural world and the divine by repeating ritual activities and symbols.

The adaptability and evolution of Wiccan practice enable it to stay meaningful and relevant in a world that is changing quickly. One of Wicca's advantages is its adaptability, which allows practitioners to add fresh perspectives, encounters, and influences to their work. Even though there are well-established Wicca lineages, such as Gardnerian and Alexandrian Wicca, the religion is fundamentally eclectic, receiving inspiration from various sources and promoting personal creativity.

The internet and digital technologies have significantly influenced the development of Wiccan practice. Social media platforms, online networks, and forums allow practitioners to interact with like-minded people, exchange expertise, and support one another. Wiccan teachings and resources are now more widely accessible thanks to virtual networking, making it more straightforward for solitary practitioners to learn about and practice the religion.

Furthermore, tolerance and diversity are becoming increasingly important in modern Wicca. The significance of establishing inclusive environments that welcome individuals from diverse backgrounds, gender identities, and sexual orientations is increasingly acknowledged by practitioners. The fundamental Wiccan principles of respect for all life and the interdependence of all entities are reflected in this inclusive approach.

Ecological sustainability and environmentalism are also essential components in contemporary Wicca. A reverence for nature is fundamental to Wicca, which translates into a dedication to safeguarding and maintaining the planet. Many Wiccans participate in environmental activism, supporting ecological justice, sustainable living, and conservation initiatives. This dedication to the earth is regarded as a holy obligation, representing the holiness of the natural world, according to Wicca.

Wicca still faces difficulties and false beliefs despite its increasing popularity and recognition. The widespread misperception and misunderstanding of Wicca in mainstream society and popular culture is one of the key obstacles. False beliefs about paganism and witchcraft can cause stigma, discrimination, and prejudice towards those who practice them. Outreach and education are essential to dispel these myths and promote a broader awareness and acceptance of Wicca and its practices.

Finding a balance between tradition and innovation presents another difficulty. Although Wicca's adaptability is one of its advantages, it may also cause division and a lack of unity within the larger society. Practitioners have to strike a balance between adopting new ideas and methods and respecting established customs.

With an eye toward the future, Wicca is likely to keep changing and adjusting to the demands and difficulties of modern society. The focus on moral conduct, environmental stewardship, and personal accountability aligns with the public's growing consciousness of global concerns, including social justice, mental health, and climate change. Wicca's comprehensive and holistic approach can provide insightful viewpoints and valuable techniques for dealing with these issues.

To sum up, the framework of Wiccan practice is flexible and varied, allowing for both coven-based and solo practices. Wicca offers a profound and significant spiritual path based on ethical magic, worshiping the God and Goddess, and reverencing nature, whether practiced alone or in a group. Wicca emphasizes community and transformation, exemplified by the responsibilities that members of a coven play and the importance of ritual and ceremony. Wicca is still a vibrant, strong tradition that offers a deep connection to the divine and the natural world as it develops further.

CHAPTER II

The Wiccan Wheel of the Year

The Sabbats: Celebrations of the Solar Cycle

Wicca's celebration of the natural world and its cycles revolves around the Sabbats. The Wheel of the Year is a collection of these eight festivals commemorated yearly to mark important dates in the solar calendar. The earth-sun link and the varying seasons are respected on the Sabbaths. They have evolved to satisfy modern spiritual demands while retaining a strong connection to ancient pagan traditions. They are rich in historical significance and have been adapted to modern Wiccan practice.

The four Greater Sabbats, derived from prehistoric Celtic celebrations, and the four Lesser Sabbats, based on the solstices and equinoxes, comprise the eight Sabbats. Every Sabbath has distinct themes, symbols, and customs representing the agricultural calendar and the cyclical aspect of life. They reflect the cycles of nature by creating a never-ending cycle of birth, development, death, and rebirth.

Celebrated on October 31st, Samhain is often regarded as the most significant Sabbat, signaling the start of the Wiccan year. Initially, a Celtic celebration signaled the harvest's end and winter's arrival. Since it was thought that there was less of a barrier between the realms of the living and the dead at this time, it was a time to pay respect to the ancestors and the spirits of the deceased. To placate stray spirits, bonfires were built, and food and drink sacrifices were offered.

Samhain is still associated with death and the ancestors in modern Wicca, but it also commemorates the life-death-rebirth cycle. It's a time for introspection, horoscopes, and remembering the dead. Some examples of rituals include candle lighting to guide the spirits, altar preparation with pictures and keepsakes of departed loved ones, and divination to seek guidance for the upcoming year. Samhain is also a time to prepare for fresh beginnings by letting go of the past.

Yule, which falls around December 21st on the Winter Solstice, commemorates the lengthiest night and the sun's rebirth. This holiday originates in several ancient cultures, such as the Roman festival of Saturnalia and the Norse celebration of the God Baldur's rebirth. Yule is when darkness gives way to light, signifying the beginning of longer days, hope, and rejuvenation.

Yule, a Wiccan holiday, commemorates the Goddess Sun God's birth, signifying the return of warmth and light. It's a season of happiness, eating, and gratitude. Daily modern Yule celebration activities include decorating a Yule tree, receiving gifts, lighting a Yule log, and having a feast with loved ones. Rituals may consist of burning candles to celebrate the sun's return and reflecting on one's growth and renewal for the upcoming year. The themes of renewal and hope are essential.

On February 1st or 2nd, Imbolc is observed, symbolizing the halfway point between the Winter Solstice and the Spring Equinox. In the past, it was a Celtic holiday honoring the Goddess Brigid, who was connected to poetry, smithing, and healing. As the first traces of new life emerge, Imbolc is a time of purification and preparation for spring.

Contemporary Wiccans observe Imbolc as a time of inspiration, cleansing, and the earth's quickening. It's a time for spiritual and bodily renewal and cleansing. Brigid's crosses, candle lighting, and cleansing rituals to make way for spring's new growth are a few examples of rites. Imbolc is also a time to take stock of oneself and make resolutions for the upcoming months.

Ostara, which falls on March 21st around the Spring Equinox, symbolizes the arrival of spring and the stability of day and night. This event, which comes from the Germanic Goddess Eostre, honors fertility, rebirth, and life blossoming. In the past, it was a time to rejoice at the passing of winter and the start of the farming season.

Ostara celebrates equilibrium, rebirth, and the earth's rising for contemporary Wicca. As the Goddess takes on her maiden form once more, marking the possibility of fresh starts and personal development, it is a moment to pay tribute to her. Planting seeds, decorating eggs, and engaging in outdoor activities to foster a connection with nature's rebirth are a few examples of rituals. Ostara is a joyful and festive occasion that heralds the return of life and the promise of plenty.

May 1st is Beltane, a celebration associated with fertility, passion, and the flowering of life. In the past, a Celtic fire celebration heralded the arrival of summer and the resurgence of life and development. Rituals were carried out to guarantee fertility and prosperity, and fires were lighted to honor the sun and to defend the community.

Beltane celebrates life, love, and fertility in contemporary Wicca. It's a moment to celebrate the union of the God and Goddess, representing nature's generative and creative powers. Maypole dance, leaping over fires for protection and purification, and feasts and music are a few examples of rituals. Beltane celebrates life's beauty and energy with joy and festivity.

Litha, which falls on June 21st around the Summer Solstice, commemorates the longest day and the sun's zenith. In the past, it was a time to praise the sun and rejoice in the earth's richness. Rituals were carried out to guarantee ongoing prosperity and protection, and bonfires were lighted as a sign of the sun's might.

Litha celebrates life's richness and the sun's light in contemporary Wicca. It's a time to celebrate the height of the growing season and express gratitude for the sun's warmth and light. Some rituals include lighting bonfires, gifting flowers and herbs, and engaging in sun meditations. Litha honors the vigor and strength of the natural world and is a time for celebration and thankfulness.

The harvest season officially begins on August 1st with Lammas, sometimes called Lughnasadh. It was once a Celtic celebration honoring the God Lugh, who was connected to artistry and talent. It was an occasion to guarantee future abundance and express gratitude for the first fruits of the crop.

Lammas is a time to appreciate the earth's richness and celebrate the first harvest in modern Wicca. It is a time to celebrate God's sacrifice to provide for our needs. Baking bread, crafting corn dollies, and engaging in acts of appreciation are a few examples of rituals. During Lammas, people give thanks and reflect, acknowledging the cycles of life and the value of community and sharing.

Mabon, which falls on September 21st during the Autumn Equinox, commemorates the second harvest and the stability of day and night. In the past, it was a time to rejoice in the earth's abundance and get ready for winter. It was a season of contemplation and gratitude, paying homage to the harmony of light and gloom.

Mabon is a time to celebrate gratitude, balance, and the harvest in modern Wicca. It's a moment to consider life's cycles and express gratitude for the earth's richness. Offering fruits and vegetables, meditating in balance, and celebrating with feasts and gatherings are a few examples of rituals. Mabon is a season of gratitude and introspection, celebrating light and dark's natural cycles and harmony.

The Sabbats have a long history derived from several old pagan customs. The Celtic festivals commemorating significant moments in the agricultural year are the source of the Greater Sabbats, including Samhain, Imbolc, Beltane, and Lammas. The intimate bond between the people and the land was reflected in these festivals, which were occasions of ritual, community, and joy. They were also transition periods, signifying the cycles of life and death and the changing seasons.

The solstices and equinoxes, astronomical phenomena observed by several cultures throughout history, constitute the foundation of the Lesser Sabbats, including Yule, Ostara, Litha, and Mabon. These celebrations pay homage to the sun's cycles and the varying seasons, which mirrors the shared human experience of coexisting peacefully with the natural world. The equinoxes and solstices, which signaled the seasons and the equilibrium of light and dark, were occasions for festivity and custom.

The agricultural calendar of ancient times was closely linked to the Sabbats, which were based on planting, growing, and harvesting cycles. These were occasions to pay homage to the gods, express gratitude for the bountiful harvest, and carry out ceremonies to guarantee prosperity and safety for all time. The festivals also served as occasions for community building, drawing people together to share, rejoice, and support one another.

The Sabbats are still very important in contemporary Wicca, offering a structure for spiritual practice and a link to the natural world. They provide an opportunity to worship the gods, celebrate life's cycles, and harmonize with the natural world's cycles. The Sabbats are periods of ritual, introspection, and festivity that present chances for personal development as well as community and a deeper relationship with God.

As the Wiccan New Year, Samhain honors the cycles of life and death and is a time for introspection and rebirth. It's a moment to respect the past, ask for wisdom for the upcoming year, and prepare for fresh starts. The main themes are death and rebirth, which represent the cycles of life.

Yule, the sun's rebirth festivity, is a season of hope and rejuvenation. It's a time to honor the natural cycles, rejoice with loved ones, and express gratitude for the sun's warmth and light. The core motifs of light and shadow and their interplay represent the shared human experience of coexisting peacefully with the natural world.

Imbolc is a time of creativity and rejuvenation as it is a season of purification and preparing for spring. It's a time to celebrate the Goddess Brigid, purify and rejuvenate, and prepare for new growth. The main themes are preparation and purification, which align with the earth's natural cycles.
Ostara is a time of rebirth and balance since it marks the start of spring. It's a moment to celebrate the earth's awakening, to recognize the harmony of light and dark, and to establish a connection with nature's cycles. Reflecting the cycles of life itself, fertility and rejuvenation are significant themes.

As the festival of passion and fertility, Beltane is a time for joy and celebration. It's a moment to celebrate life and love, pay homage to the marriage of God and Goddess, and establish a connection with the regenerative powers of the natural world. The primary themes are desire and fertility, representing the cycles of growth and life.

Litha is a season of thanksgiving and gladness since it honors the sun's power. It's a time to enjoy the height of the growing season, express gratitude for the sun's warmth and brightness, and establish a connection with the natural world. The fundamental themes of vigor and power mirror the cycles of life.

As the festival of the first crop, Lammas is a season of contemplation and gratitude. It's a moment to recognize God's sacrifice, express gratitude for the planet's bounty, and prepare for the upcoming months. Harvest and abundance are significant themes that highlight the value of community and sharing and life's natural cycles.

Mabon is a season of thanksgiving and introspection since it commemorates the equilibrium of day and night. It's a time to appreciate the harmony of light and dark, express gratitude for the earth's wealth, and prepare for winter. The fundamental concepts of thankfulness and balance represent all things' interdependence and nature's cycles.

Providing a structure for spiritual practice and a link to the natural world, the Sabbats are essential to Wiccan rituals. They offer the opportunity to worship the gods, celebrate life's cycles, and harmonize with the natural world's cycles. The Sabbats are periods of ritual, introspection, and festivity that present chances for personal development as well as community and a deeper relationship with God. Wiccans can connect with the old traditions of their ancestors through the Sabbath celebrations while modifying and modernizing their practices to suit contemporary demands.

The Esbats: Honoring the Lunar Cycle

The Esbats are revered Wicca events arranged to commemorate the Moon's phases, especially the new and full moons. These rites are essential to Wiccan practice because the Moon phase is a powerful symbol of the Goddess and life's cycles. The cycles of birth, growth, maturity, decline, and rebirth are reflected in the phases of the Moon, which go from new to waxing, full, waning, and back to new. Moon phases offer distinct energies that can be used for various magical and spiritual endeavors. Wiccans use Esbat ceremonies to better connect with the divine feminine, strengthen their spiritual practices and harmonize with these moon energies.

In Wiccan tradition, the full Moon is the most joyous phase, frequently seen as the zenith of the Moon's force and impact. The Moon is lit during a full moon, signifying increased spiritual energy, clarity, and fullness. Esbats, or full moon rites, are occasions for joy, thanksgiving, and potent magical operations. Wiccans assemble under the full Moon to pay homage to the Goddess, who is frequently said to be at her most powerful during this period. Many other rituals can be carried out, including divination, offering-making, and spell-casting.

Traditionally, full moon rituals start with casting a sacred circle, which helps center the participants' energies and establishes a safe area for the ceremony. The four elements—Earth, Air, Fire, and Water—are called upon to energize and balance the area when the circle is formed, usually using a wand or an athame (a ceremonial knife). After the circle is formed, the Moon is called upon, usually by a chant or prayer that summons the Goddess and extends an invitation for her to enter the circle. This invocation, which aims to create a direct line of communication between the participants and the holy, has the potential to be incredibly moving.

Depending on the particular topic of the Esbat, different rituals may be carried out following the invocation. Offerings to the Goddess, including food, flowers, or herbs; prayers and meditations; and the execution of magical deeds are a few examples of these rites. When the Moon is full, magic is said to be particularly powerful since the Moon's energy is at its highest. Spells for abundance, protection, and healing are frequently used during full moon esbats, as are divination techniques like scrying and tarot reading.

Conversely, the new Moon symbolizes possibilities for development and fresh starts. The new Moon signifies the beginning of a new cycle and is a time for making intentions and sowing seeds for the future. In contrast, the full Moon is a time for celebration and conclusion. Therefore, the focus of new moon ceremonies is on introspection, goal-setting, and the start of new endeavors. New moon Esbats start with casting a holy circle and the moon's invocation, just as full moon rites. Nonetheless, the new Moon's more reflective and subdued energy offers a chance for in-depth introspection and reflection.

Participants in new moon ceremonies frequently take part in exercises that assist them in defining their objectives and setting aspirations for the upcoming lunar cycle. This can involve keeping a journal, making vision boards, or engaging in meditations to help individuals connect with their inner goals and objectives. The new Moon is also a potent period for shadow work, which is the exploration and healing of one's own hidden or repressed qualities. Wiccans aim to utilize this phase's natural potential for growth and transformation by working with the energies of the new Moon.

Wiccans employ the energy and influences of the Moon's new, waxing, full, waning, and dark phases in their magical practices. The time between the new and full moons is known as the waxing Moon, and it symbolizes development, expansion, and rising vitality. Spells and rituals that promote wealth, attractiveness, and resource accumulation are best performed during this time. Wiccans may conduct rituals to draw in love, prosperity, or fresh possibilities during the waxing Moon since the Moon's increased light represents the strength of their aspirations.

The time between the new and full moons is known as the waning Moon, and it is symbolic of reflection, release, and decline. This stage is appropriate for rituals and spells, including cleansing, letting go, and banishing. Wiccans may carry out rituals to cleanse their homes and sacred spaces, let go of bad habits, and drive out harmful influences during the declining Moon. The Moon is an excellent symbol of introspection and spiritual cleansing since its waning light represents the process of shedding and purification.

The black Moon, the time before the new Moon when the Moon is not visible in the sky, signifies the last phase of the lunar cycle and is a suitable moment for introspection and relaxation. Dark moon rituals frequently center on contemplation, meditation, and connecting with the most enigmatic and concealed facets of the divine. To prepare for the new cycle that starts with the new Moon, practitioners might use this period for silent reflection and spiritual rejuvenation.

The moon's phases fundamentally influence Wiccan practice since each one gives unique energies that can be used for particular reasons. Wiccans aim to enhance the efficacy of their magical practices by harmonizing their rituals and spells with the lunar phases, fostering harmony with the inherent cycles of the cosmos. Given that the Moon is seen as a potent emblem of the Goddess and her capacity for constant change, this lunar alignment also helps to strengthen their relationship with the divine.

With its bright and potent energy, the full Moon is frequently utilized for spells that require strength and clarity. For instance, healing spells are often cast during a full moon since the intense light is thought to enhance the healing energies and provide clarity to the healing process. Spells for protection work particularly well with a full moon since the light represents the energy that wards off evil forces.

Another widespread practice during the full Moon is divination since the increased energy is supposed to improve psychic and intuitive powers. Tools like scrying mirrors, runes, and tarot cards are frequently employed during full moon ceremonies to obtain wisdom and direction. The full moon's clarity and brilliance facilitate the opening of spiritual vision and the disclosure of hidden truths.

The peaceful, contemplative energy of the new Moon makes it perfect for spells and rituals that center around fresh starts and personal development. Now is the moment to plan and sow the seeds for the following projects. During the new Moon, spells intended to express desires, initiate new projects, or attract new possibilities are most effective. The new Moon's hidden and gloomy qualities enable practitioners to explore their subconscious when the moon increases in power and light during the waxing moon and heal unresolved difficulties.

During the waxing Moon, when the Moon increases in power and light, Wiccans frequently cast spells to draw in and accumulate resources. Spells focused on love, prosperity, or personal growth work best during this phase. Growing light signifies expansion and growth; therefore, now is a great time to attract abundance and positive energy.

With its dwindling light, the waning Moon is a time for releasing and banishing. During this period, spells that break bad habits, eliminate impediments, or cleanse and purify work best. The energy of the waning Moon facilitates the process of parting with what is no longer required, enabling spiritual rebirth and purification.

The black Moon is a time for profound reflection and spiritual rejuvenation, even though it is not as frequently utilized for active spellwork. It is a time for introspection and relaxation, enabling practitioners to replenish their energies and prepare for the next cycle. Meditation, self-healing, and developing a deeper connection to the divine's mysteries are some of the topics covered in dark moon ceremonies. This phase prepares the ground for the new beginnings of the next lunar cycle by serving as a period of spiritual rest and preparation.

Wicca's use of the moon phases in magic has significant symbolic meaning and is a helpful tool. The life, death, and rebirth cycles of the Moon serve as a reminder to practitioners of the universal laws of nature that govern all things. Wiccans aim to improve their spiritual practices and strengthen their relationship with the divine by working with these cycles to align themselves considerable energies of the universe.

Besides the practical applications of lunar magic, Wicca places great symbolic value on the Moon. Many people regard the Moon as a symbol of the Goddess, representing her cyclical and ever-changing nature. The Moon's phases symbolize the various facets of the Goddess: the dark Moon symbolizes the hidden and enigmatic side of the divine feminine; the full Moon the mature mother; the waning Moon the wise crone; and the new Moon the virgin.

Lunar magic gains a deep spiritual component from this symbolic relationship between the Goddess and the Moon. In addition to utilizing the Moon's beneficial powers, Wiccans regenerates the divine feminine and her cyclical nature by conducting rituals and spells by phases. This alignment enhances their practice's spiritual and transformative qualities by fostering a closer relationship with the Goddess and the natural world.

Wiccans are also linked to the natural rhythms of the earth and the universe through the observance of the lunar cycle and the celebration of the Esbats. These rituals offer a means of reestablishing a connection with the natural world and living in balance with its cycles in a society that frequently feels cut off from it. The Moon provides a physical reminder of life's cycles and the value of coexisting peacefully with the environment through its regular and predictable phases.

The Esbats are very important to Wiccan practice since they offer a structure for respecting the lunar cycle and using its energy for magical and spiritual development. Wiccans establish a close connection with the divine feminine force represented by the Moon through rituals performed throughout the new and complete moon phases, which mirror the Moon's impact on the natural world and human consciousness. Full moon rituals are perfect for achieving clarity, goal fulfillment, and spiritual enlightenment since they occur during increased energy, illumination, and manifestation. On the other hand, reflection, fresh starts, and intention-setting are the main themes of new moon rituals, which align with the moon's dark phase and growth potential. With the help of the natural cycles, every phase of the Moon—waxing, full, waning, and new—offers unique chances for magical operations and introspective growth. Wiccans develop a deeper awareness of themselves and their role in the cosmos by coordinating their activities with the phases of the Moon. This also helps them to strengthen their spiritual bond. Because of this, the Esbats are revered times for introspection, rebirth, and empowerment. They enable practitioners to integrate with nature and channel its energies to positively change their personal and communal lives.

Seasonal Practices and Traditions

Humanity's bond with nature and its cycles is fundamental to seasonal customs and activities. These customs, which have evolved over millennia, demonstrate a deep awareness of the natural environment and our place in it. Communities and individuals can become attuned to the earth's rhythms by aligning with natural cycles, promoting balance and harmony. Creating individual and collective rituals pays homage to these age-old customs in this setting. It fosters a sense of continuity and community in a world that is becoming increasingly fractured.

Spring, summer, fall, and winter are the four main seasons around which seasonal activities usually revolve. Every season has unique qualities, difficulties, and possibilities that impact daily routines, cultural customs, and agricultural activities. For instance, spring is a season of rebirth and rejuvenation. People rejoice for the revival of growth and vitality as the earth emerges from its winter hibernation. Festivals and ceremonies honoring the land's fertility and the arrival of warmer weather are observed on this day in many cultures. Symbolizing new beginnings and growth potential, everyday rituals around this season include cleaning homes, planting seeds, and participating in outdoor activities.

Summertime is frequently linked to festivity and plenty because of its long days and copious amounts of sunlight. Gatherings of the community and the harvest are customary during this season. Celebrations of all kinds, including fairs, festivals, and group dinners, highlight the value of ties to the community and similar experiences. Summertime brings a lively, energetic vibe that invites individuals to interact with each other and their environment. Several outdoor customs honor the sun's warmth and the pinnacle of the earth's fertility, including bonfires, dances, and music.

Autumn is a season for introspection and thankfulness as the days get shorter and the harvest nears its end. The emphasis switches from external activities to introspection. Thanksgiving rituals and harvest festivals are customary celebrations praising the earth's abundance and the toil of the producing season. It's also a time to be spiritually and physically ready for the following winter. In tandem with tasks like food preservation, firewood gathering, and clothing repair, some rituals promote reflection and creating goals for the upcoming months.

Winter is a time for relaxation and renewal because of its cold and darkness. This is the moment to practice energy and resource conservation on a personal and a community level. Despite the terrible weather outside, many cultures have customs involving storytelling, dining, and other inside activities promoting warmth and community. The return of light is a common theme in celebrations of the winter solstice, which falls on the longest night of the year and represents optimism and the possibility of rebirth. A solid connection to one's inner self and the cyclical aspect of existence is encouraged throughout this season.

A potent method to foster relationships with the environment and one another is to time individual and collective rituals by these natural cycles. Journaling, meditation, or artistic endeavors that evoke the season's themes might be examples of personal rituals. For instance, in the spring, one may make it a regular habit to observe how the natural world is changing, and in the fall, one might concentrate on reviewing the year's accomplishments and making plans for the future. By encouraging mindfulness of the natural environment and the present moment, these rituals aid in developing balance and serenity in people.

Group rituals, however, place more of an emphasis on shared experiences and community. Seasonal events allow people to get together and celebrate their relationship to the planet and one another, such as harvest festivals, solstice parties, and potluck dinners. Seasonal activities like planting trees in the spring, having a community meal in the summer, offering gratitude in the fall, and burning candles in the winter are frequently a part of these gatherings. These customs foster a sense of purpose and belonging among all group members and strengthen social ties.

Developing these rituals can serve as a way to reflect modern ideas while still preserving tradition. Numerous contemporary seasonal customs are reimagined traditions with fresh significance. For example, Earth Day, a springtime celebration, is a modern spin on traditional festivals honoring the fertility of the earth, with an emphasis on environmental protection and awareness. Similarly, community-supported agriculture (CSA) initiatives promote a sense of connection to the land and the surrounding community by emulating old communal agricultural techniques through workdays and seasonal festivities.

Understanding and committing to coexist with the natural world are prerequisites for implementing these principles into daily life. Understanding the rhythms of life can be gained by keeping an eye on changes in the natural world, such as the length of the days, the phases of the moon, and the actions of plants and animals. This awareness can help people make decisions and follow daily routines harmonizing with the environment. Eating foods that are in season and locally obtained, for instance, supports local farmers, lowers carbon emissions, and corresponds with nature's growing and harvest cycles.

Creating rituals, both individually and collectively, calls for imagination and purpose. It is a chance to consider what is significant and to develop behaviors that uphold those ideals. This could entail investigating old traditions and modifying them to fit modern living, or it could entail developing brand-new rituals that speak to the experiences and goals of today. The secret is to embrace these practices mindfully and with reverence, understanding the deeper connections they stand for.

Many civilizations identify other cycles and transitions within the year besides the four main seasons. For instance, the midpoints of the solstices and equinoxes are marked by festivals like Imbolc, Beltane, Lughnasadh, and Samhain in the Celtic tradition. These holidays offer more chances for ritual and celebration while drawing attention to the minute changes in the natural world. Early February is Imbolc, a period for purification and cleaning in preparation for the arrival of spring. Early May sees the celebration of Beltane, a time when flowers begin to bloom and fecundity. Samhain, observed at the end of October, commemorates the conclusion of the harvest and the onset of winter. It is celebrated with ceremonies that honor the ancestors and the cycle of life and death. Lughnasadh, celebrated in early August, heralds the start of the harvest season.

These extra cycles can strengthen the bond with nature and offer a more comprehensive framework for individual and collective rituals. For each of these festivals, a person may establish a particular ritual. For example, at Imbolc, they might light a candle and make intentions; at Beltane, they might make a flower crown and dance. Similarly, a community might schedule seasonal get-togethers with events like storytelling, meal sharing, and tree planting to foster continuity and a sense of purpose all year.

Ultimately, cultivating a sense of harmony and connectedness is the ultimate goal of creating personal and communal rituals and timing oneself with the cycles of nature. It is an acknowledgment that the cycles of the planet and the universe impact us as members of a broader web of life. By recognizing and implementing significant customs that mirror these cycles, people and societies can develop a more profound feeling of inclusion and direction. This can result in a more contented and sustainable style of living that is in balance with the natural world and the more significant cycles of life.

To sum up, seasonal customs and rituals provide a meaningful means of fostering relationships between the natural world and one another. People can establish balance, continuity, and direction in their lives and communities by coordinating personal and collective rituals with the natural cycles. These customs honor the earth's rhythms and the deeper connections they symbolize. They are derived from old traditions and modified for modern living. Engaging with these seasonal cycles, whether via introspection, group celebration, or artistic expression, promotes a sense of community and belonging that benefits people's lives and the broader one.

CHAPTER III

Tools and Symbols in Wiccan Practice

The Altar: A Sacred Space

The concept of an altar as a sacred space holds profound significance across various cultures and religious traditions. An altar is a focal point for worship, reflection, and connection with the divine. It is a space imbued with spiritual energy, dedicated to ritual practices and the veneration of deities, ancestors, or universal principles. The altar's physical and symbolic aspects contribute to its role as a conduit for spiritual communication and a sanctuary for personal and communal devotion.

An altar's physical composition varies widely depending on cultural and religious contexts. In many traditions, an altar is a carefully arranged structure adorned with symbols, icons, and offerings. These elements serve as tangible representations of spiritual beliefs and aspirations. For instance, in Christian traditions, an altar in a church often features a cross, candles, and sacred texts, reflecting the central themes of sacrifice and redemption. In Hindu households, a home altar may include statues or images of deities, incense, flowers, and food offerings, symbolizing devotion and hospitality to the divine.

An altar arrangement is often guided by principles that reflect the underlying spiritual worldview. The placement of objects, the choice of materials, and the use of colors all carry symbolic meanings. In Feng Shui, a Chinese practice of harmonizing individuals with their environment, the orientation and elements of an altar are meticulously chosen to promote balance and positive energy flow. Similarly, in indigenous traditions, altars are constructed using natural materials like stones, wood, and plants, emphasizing the connection between the sacred space and the natural world.

Beyond its physical attributes, an altar holds profound symbolic significance. It is a microcosm of the universe, where the material and spiritual realms intersect. Creating and maintaining an altar is a spiritual practice that fosters mindfulness, intention, and reverence. Each object on the altar carries symbolic weight and serves as a reminder of spiritual values and commitments. For example, a candle represents illumination and the presence of the divine, while an offering of food signifies gratitude and the sustenance provided by the earth.

Altars also play a crucial role in ritual practices. Rituals performed at the altar can range from simple daily offerings and prayers to elaborate ceremonies involving multiple participants. These rituals are acts of devotion that reinforce spiritual beliefs and create a sense of continuity with tradition. In many cultures, rituals at the altar mark significant life events such as births, marriages, and deaths, serving as communal rites of passage that bind individuals to their community and heritage. For example, in the Jewish tradition, the Sabbath meal is often conducted at a home altar, where blessings are recited, and candles are lit to usher in the sacred time of rest and reflection.

The personal altar, often found in individual homes, serves as a private reflection and meditation sanctuary. It is a place where individuals can retreat from the distractions of daily life and reconnect with their inner selves. The personal altar is highly individualized, reflecting its creator's unique spiritual journey and aspirations. It may include items of personal significance, such as photographs of loved ones, mementos from significant life events, or objects that evoke a sense of peace and inspiration. This intimate space becomes a focal point for personal rituals, such as journaling, prayer, or contemplation, providing a sense of grounding and spiritual nourishment.

In addition to their role in personal and communal worship, altars also function as spaces of healing and transformation. Many traditions believe that an altar can serve as a portal for divine intervention and blessings. Making offerings, lighting candles, or reciting prayers at the altar is a way to invoke spiritual assistance and protection. In times of crisis or illness, an altar becomes a place of solace where individuals can seek comfort and guidance. Engaging with the altar—placing an offering, lighting a candle, or praying—can be therapeutic, helping individuals cope with challenges and find inner strength.

Altars are also dynamic spaces that evolve, reflecting the ongoing spiritual journey of individuals and communities. As circumstances change and new insights are gained, the altar can be rearranged or refreshed to represent new intentions and aspirations. This dynamic quality allows the altar to remain a relevant and living part of spiritual practice. For example, during significant religious festivals or seasonal transitions, an altar might be decorated with specific symbols and offerings that correspond to the themes of the occasion. This adaptability ensures that the altar remains a vibrant and meaningful space that resonates with its practitioners' current spiritual needs and experiences.

Moreover, the altar serves as a powerful symbol of interconnectedness. It is a place where the individual meets the universal, where personal intentions and prayers are offered up to a higher power or the collective consciousness. This interconnectedness is especially evident in communal altars, which unite people in shared worship and celebration. The communal altar becomes a focal point for collective rituals and ceremonies, fostering a sense of unity and belonging. In Indigenous cultures, for instance, community altars are often used in ceremonies that honor the land, ancestors, and spirits, reinforcing the bonds between people, their heritage, and the natural world.

In contemporary contexts, the concept of an altar has expanded to include non-religious and secular interpretations. Many people create altars for personal reflection, creativity, and intention-setting. These modern altars might consist of vision boards, inspirational quotes, and objects representing personal goals and values. Engaging with these altars can be a form of mindfulness practice, helping individuals focus their thoughts and energies on what matters most to them. This secular adaptation of the altar demonstrates its enduring relevance as a tool for fostering connection, intention, and transformation.

In conclusion, the altar as a sacred space is significant across various cultural and religious traditions. It is a physical and symbolic focal point for worship, reflection, and spiritual practice. The creation and maintenance of an altar foster mindfulness, intention, and reverence, while rituals performed at the altar reinforce spiritual beliefs and create a sense of continuity with tradition. Personal altars provide a sanctuary for private reflection, while communal altars foster a sense of unity and belonging. In traditional or contemporary contexts, the altar remains a powerful symbol of interconnectedness and a dynamic space for spiritual engagement and transformation.

The Elements and Elemental Tools

The four classical elements—Earth, Air, Fire, and Water—have been fundamental concepts in various philosophical, spiritual, and scientific traditions throughout history. Each element represents different aspects of the natural world and human experience, embodying unique qualities and energies. In many magical and spiritual practices, these elements are symbolized by specific tools: the pentacle for Earth, the athame for Air, the wand for Fire, and the chalice for Water. This section explores the significance of these elements and their corresponding tools, examining their historical roots, symbolic meanings, and practical uses in rituals and meditations.

Earth is often associated with stability, grounding, and physicality. It represents life's tangible, material aspects, such as the body, health, wealth, and the environment. The Earth element is seen as nurturing and sustaining, providing the foundation upon which all life depends. It is connected to the North, the winter season, and the color green. In many traditions, Earth is considered feminine, embodying fertility, growth, and receptivity.

The pentacle, a five-pointed star enclosed in a circle, is the tool that represents Earth. Each point of the star corresponds to the elements of Earth, Air, Fire, Water, and Spirit, while the circle symbolizes unity and wholeness. The pentacle is a protective symbol, often used to ward off negative energies and create a sacred space. In magical practices, it invokes the Earth element, grounding energies, and focusing intent. The pentacle can be used in various rituals for prosperity, healing, and protection as a physical reminder of the practitioner's connection to the Earth.

Air, in contrast, is associated with intellect, communication, and the mind. It represents the intangible, unseen forces influencing our thoughts, ideas, and interactions. Air is connected to the East, the spring season, and the color yellow. It is often considered masculine, embodying clarity, precision, and swiftness. The element of Air governs the realms of knowledge, inspiration, and creativity, making it essential for activities that involve planning, strategizing, and problem-solving.

The athame, a double-edged ritual knife, symbolizes the element of Air. Traditionally, the athame is not used for physical cutting but for directing and controlling energy. Its sharp blade represents the clarity and precision of thought and the ability to cut through illusions and reveal truth. In rituals, the athame is often used to cast and close the circle, invoking protective boundaries and defining sacred space. It can also be employed in spells and meditations that involve communication, study, or mental clarity. By wielding the athame, practitioners harness the power of Air to enhance their intellectual and communicative abilities.

Fire, the element of transformation, passion, and will, is the most dynamic and volatile of the four. It symbolizes the force of creation and destruction, the spark of life, and the drive to achieve and conquer. Fire is connected to the South, the summer season, and red. It is often seen as masculine, embodying strength, courage, and determination. The element of Fire governs the realms of action, energy, and desire, making it crucial for pursuits that require motivation, initiative, and leadership.

The wand, a slender rod often made from wood, represents the element of Fire. The wand serves as a conduit for directing willpower and energy, much like the athame, but with a focus on creation and manifestation rather than intellect and clarity. In rituals, the wand is used to channel and amplify the practitioner's intent, whether casting spells, invoking deities, or drawing symbols in the Air. It can be employed in various magical workings, particularly passion, creativity, and transformation. The wand's connection to Fire empowers practitioners to ignite their inner flame and pursue their goals with vigor and enthusiasm.

Water, the element of emotions, intuition, and the subconscious, is associated with fluidity, adaptability, and depth. It represents the flow of feelings and the ever-changing nature of the emotional landscape. Water is connected to the West, the autumn season, and the color blue. It is often considered feminine, embodying compassion, empathy, and intuition. The element of Water governs the realms of relationships, dreams, and psychic abilities, making it essential for activities that involve healing, nurturing, and emotional exploration.

The chalice, a cup or goblet, symbolizes the element of Water. The chalice represents the receptive and nurturing aspects of the feminine, as well as the ability to contain and channel emotions. In rituals, the chalice is often used to hold Water, wine, or other liquids, serving as a focal point for blessings, libations, and offerings. It can also be employed in spells and meditations that involve love, healing, and psychic development. By working with the chalice, practitioners connect with the depth of their emotions and intuition, enhancing their ability to navigate the currents of their inner world.

These elements' interplay and corresponding tools form the foundation of many magical and spiritual practices. Each component offers unique qualities and energies that can be harnessed for personal growth, healing, and transformation. By working with the pentacle, athame, wand, and chalice, practitioners can create a balanced and harmonious approach to their spiritual journey, integrating the physical, mental, emotional, and energetic aspects of their being.

In addition to their significance, the elements and their tools often work together in rituals to create a cohesive and robust experience. For example, a ritual might begin with casting a circle using the athame, invoking the protection and clarity of Air. The practitioner might then use the pentacle to ground and center themselves, drawing upon Earth's stability and nurturing energy. The wand could be employed to set intentions and ignite the passion and will of Fire, while the chalice might be used to offer blessings and connect with the intuitive and emotional depths of Water. This holistic approach ensures that all aspects of the practitioner's being are engaged and balanced, facilitating a more profound and more effective spiritual practice.

Historically, the concept of the four elements can be traced back to ancient civilizations such as Greece, Egypt, and India. The Greek philosopher Empedocles is often credited with formalizing the theory of the four classical elements in the 5th century BCE. He proposed that all matter is composed of Earth, Air, Fire, and Water and that these elements are in constant interplay, creating the diverse phenomena of the natural world. This idea was further developed by later philosophers such as Plato and Aristotle, who explored the qualities and relationships of the elements in their works.

In Egypt, the elements were associated with different deities and aspects of creation. For example, the god Geb was linked to Earth, the goddess Nut to Air, Ra to Fire, and Tefnut to Water. These associations reflected the Egyptians' understanding of the elements as fundamental forces of nature, each governed by divine beings. Similarly, in Hinduism, the elements are known as the "Pancha Mahabhutas" and are considered essential components of the cosmos. The elements are associated with different deities and aspects of the self, emphasizing their importance in both the external and internal worlds.

The use of elemental tools in magical practices can be found in various traditions, including Wicca, ceremonial magic, and shamanism. In Wicca, for instance, the elements and their tools are central to rituals and spellwork. The pentacle, athame, wand, and chalice are often placed on the altar, representing the presence and influence of the elements. These tools are used in various ways, such as casting circles, invoking deities, and performing spells, each drawing upon the associated element's specific qualities.

Ceremonial magic, which has its roots in the Western esoteric tradition, also emphasizes using elemental tools. Practitioners might employ the tools in complex rituals designed to invoke elemental forces, align with planetary energies, or communicate with spiritual entities. The precise use of the tools, combined with elaborate ritual structures and symbolic gestures, allows practitioners to harness the power of the elements in a focused and controlled manner.

In shamanic traditions, the elements are often viewed as living spirits or energies that can be interacted with and called upon for guidance and healing. Shamans might use objects such as stones, feathers, Fire, and Water in their rituals to represent and connect with the elements. These practices emphasize the importance of maintaining harmony and balance with the natural world, recognizing the interconnectedness of all things.

In conclusion, the four elements—Earth, Air, Fire, and Water—are foundational concepts in many spiritual and magical traditions. Each element embodies unique qualities and energies, offering valuable insights and tools for personal growth and transformation. The pentacle, athame, wand, and chalice are tangible representations of these elements, providing practitioners with a means to connect with and harness their power. By working with these tools and elements, individuals can create a balanced and harmonious approach to their spiritual practice, integrating the physical, mental, emotional, and energetic aspects of their being. This holistic approach enriches their personal journey and fosters a deeper connection with the natural world and the universal forces that shape our existence.

Sacred Symbols and Their Meanings

Symbols have always held significant power in human culture as bridges between the mundane and the sacred. In Wiccan art and ritual, symbols play a crucial role, serving as tools for focus, protection, and the embodiment of spiritual principles. The pentagram stands out as one of the most recognizable and meaningful symbols among these. This section explores the pentagram and other vital symbols in Wiccan practice, delving into their historical roots, symbolic meanings, and practical ritual application.

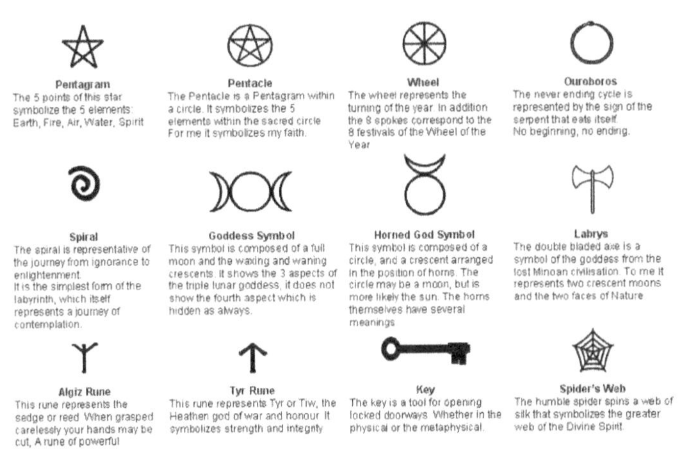

Pentagram
The 5 points of this star symbolize the 5 elements: Earth, Fire, Air, Water, Spirit

Pentacle
The Pentacle is a Pentagram within a circle. It symbolizes the 5 elements within the sacred circle. For me it symbolizes my faith.

Wheel
The wheel represents the turning of the year. In addition the 8 spokes correspond to the 8 festivals of the Wheel of the Year

Ouroboros
The never ending cycle is represented by the sign of the serpent that eats itself. No beginning, no ending.

Spiral
The spiral is representative of the journey from ignorance to enlightenment. It is the simplest form of the labyrinth, which itself represents a journey of contemplation.

Goddess Symbol
This symbol is composed of a full moon and the waxing and waning crescents. It shows the 3 aspects of the triple lunar goddess, it does not show the fourth aspect which is hidden as always.

Horned God Symbol
This symbol is composed of a circle, and a crescent arranged in the position of horns. The circle may be a moon, but is more likely the sun. The horns themselves have several meanings

Labrys
The double bladed axe is a symbol of the goddess from the lost Minoan civilisation. To me it represents two crescent moons and the two faces of Nature

Algiz Rune
This rune represents the sedge or reed. When grasped carelessly your hands may be cut, A rune of powerful protection.

Tyr Rune
This rune represents Tyr or Tiw, the Heathen god of war and honour. It symbolizes strength and integrity

Key
The key is a tool for opening locked doorways. Whether in the physical or the metaphysical.

Spider's Web
The humble spider spins a web of silk that symbolizes the greater web of the Divine Spirit.

The pentagram, a five-pointed star often enclosed in a circle, is one of the most potent symbols in the Wiccan tradition. Its history stretches back to ancient civilizations, including the Greeks and Egyptians, where it was associated with various deities and cosmic principles. In Wicca, the pentagram represents the five elements: Earth, Air, Fire, Water, and Spirit. Each point of the star corresponds to one of these elements, with the uppermost point symbolizing Spirit, the unifying force that connects and transcends the physical elements. The surrounding circle signifies wholeness and the cyclical nature of life, emphasizing the interconnectedness of all things.

In rituals, the pentagram is often used for protection and invocation. Drawing a pentagram in the Air with a ritual knife or athame can help create a protective barrier, shielding the practitioner from negative energies. Visualizing the pentagram can aid in focusing intent and connecting with the elemental forces when performing spells or meditations. Additionally, the pentagram is commonly worn as a pendant or amulet, serving as a personal symbol of faith and protection.

Another significant symbol in Wiccan art and ritual is the triple moon, which consists of three lunar phases: waxing crescent, full moon, and waning crescent. This symbol represents the Triple Goddess, a central figure in Wiccan theology. The Triple Goddess embodies the three stages of a woman's life: the Maiden, the Mother, and the Crone. Each moon phase corresponds to one of these aspects, with the waxing crescent representing the Maiden, symbolizing youth, new beginnings, and growth. The full moon represents the Mother, embodying fertility, maturity, and nurturing. The waning crescent represents the Crone, symbolizing wisdom, introspection, and endings.

The triple moon is often used in rituals to invoke the presence and guidance of the Triple Goddess. It can be displayed on altars, worn as jewelry, or incorporated into ritual tools. By connecting with the energy of the Triple Goddess, practitioners seek to balance the different aspects of their lives and tap into the cyclical wisdom of the lunar phases.

The ankh, an ancient Egyptian symbol resembling a cross with a loop at the top, also holds significance in Wiccan practice. Known as the "key of life," the ankh represents eternal life, fertility, and the union of opposites. Its shape combines masculine and feminine principles, with the vertical line symbolizing the phallus and the loop representing the womb. In Wiccan rituals, the ankh can invoke the divine's life-giving energies and promote balance and harmony between different aspects of existence.

The ankh is often worn as a talisman for protection and vitality. Its presence in rituals can enhance the flow of life force energy, aiding in healing and spiritual rejuvenation. By incorporating the ankh into their practices, Wiccans connect with the ancient wisdom of Egypt and the universal principles of life and death.

The spiral is another powerful symbol in Wiccan art and ritual. This shape, found in nature in shells, galaxies, and weather patterns, represents growth, evolution, and the cyclical nature of life. The spiral is often associated with the Goddess, symbolizing her ever-changing and evolving nature. In rituals, drawing or visualizing a spiral can aid in connecting with the divine feminine and the processes of transformation and regeneration.

Spirals are frequently used in meditation and pathworking, guiding practitioners through the layers of their consciousness and facilitating deep introspection. They can also be incorporated into the design of ritual spaces, such as labyrinths, to create a sacred journey towards inner understanding and spiritual enlightenment. By working with the spiral, Wiccans align themselves with the natural rhythms of the universe and the continual process of becoming.

The pentacle, which differs slightly from the pentagram in that it is the five-pointed star within a circle, is another important symbol in Wiccan practice. The pentacle is often made from natural materials like wood or metal and is used for grounding and protection. It can be placed on the altar to represent the element of Earth and anchor the ritual space's energies. The pentacle is a focal point during ceremonies, helping concentrate and direct the practitioner's intentions.

In addition to its ritual uses, the pentacle symbolizes the practitioner's faith and commitment to the Wiccan path. It can be worn as jewelry or displayed in the home to signify dedication to harmony, balance, and respect for nature. The pentacle's enduring power lies in connecting the practitioner with the elemental forces and the greater spiritual realities underpinning the material world.

The triquetra, a three-cornered knot, is another significant symbol in Wicca. It represents the triplicity of life, often interpreted as the Triple Goddess (Maiden, Mother, Crone), the three realms (Land, Sea, Sky), or the interconnectedness of mind, body, and Spirit. The triquetra's endless knot design also signifies eternity and the interconnectedness of all existence. In Wiccan rituals, the triquetra can invoke the presence of the Triple Goddess or emphasize the unity of different aspects of life.

The triquetra is often incorporated into ritual tools, jewelry, and artwork. Its presence serves as a reminder of the interconnected nature of reality and the importance of balancing different aspects of one's life. By working with the triquetra, practitioners can deepen their understanding of the cycles and patterns that shape their spiritual journey.

The athame, a ritual knife, is a tool and a symbol in Wiccan practice. Traditionally, the athame has a double-edged blade and a black handle. It represents the element of Air and is used to direct energy, cast circles, and invoke deities. The athame is not used for physical cutting but for cutting energetic ties and boundaries. Its sharp blade symbolizes clarity, precision, and the power of the mind to shape reality.

In rituals, the athame is often used to define the sacred space by casting the circle. It can also be employed in spellwork to channel and focus intent, ensuring the practitioner's will is directed towards their desired outcome. The athame's presence in Wiccan practice highlights the importance of mental clarity and the power of thought in manifesting change.

The wand is another essential tool and symbol in the Wiccan ritual. Typically made from wood, the wand represents the element of Fire and is used to channel and direct energy. It can cast circles, invoke spirits, and charge objects with magical intent. The wand's association with Fire emphasizes its role in transformation and the manifestation of will.

In rituals, the wand is often used to draw symbols in the Air or on the ground, creating pathways for energy to flow. It can also bless and consecrate objects, infusing them with the practitioner's intent. The wand's presence in Wiccan practice underscores the importance of focused will and the transformative power of Fire in spiritual work.

The chalice, a cup or goblet, represents the element of Water and is used in rituals to hold liquid offerings, such as Water, wine, or herbal infusions. The chalice symbolizes the receptive, nurturing aspects of the divine feminine and is often associated with the Goddess. In rituals, the chalice can invoke Water's energies, facilitating emotional healing, intuition, and connection with the subconscious.

The chalice is often placed on the altar and used in rituals involving libations, blessings, and scrying. Its presence in Wiccan practice highlights the importance of receptivity, compassion, and emotional depth. By working with the chalice, practitioners can enhance their connection with the intuitive and nurturing aspects of their being.

The cauldron, a pot or kettle used for cooking and brewing, is another significant symbol in the Wiccan ritual. It represents the element of Water and the transformative power of the Goddess. The cauldron is often used in rituals to brew potions, burn incense, or hold sacred fires. Its association with transformation and rebirth makes it a powerful tool for rituals involving healing, divination, and manifestation.

In Wiccan mythology, the cauldron is often associated with the Celtic Goddess Cerridwen, who possesses a magical cauldron of inspiration and transformation. In rituals, the cauldron can symbolize the womb of the Goddess, the source of all creation and renewal. By working with the cauldron, practitioners can tap into the transformative energies of the divine feminine and the cycles of birth, death, and rebirth.

The besom, or broom, is another important symbol in Wiccan practice. Traditionally made from natural materials, the besom represents the element of Air and is used to cleanse and purify ritual spaces. The act of sweeping with the besom symbolizes the removal of negative energies and the preparation of a sacred space for ritual work.

In rituals, the besom can symbolically sweep away unwanted influences and create a clean, energized space for magical work. It is also associated with the idea of traveling between worlds, as witches were often depicted riding broomsticks in folklore. By working with the besom, practitioners can enhance their ability to purify and protect their sacred spaces.

In conclusion, sacred symbols and their meanings are integral to Wiccan art and ritual, providing practitioners with powerful tools for focus, protection, and spiritual connection. The pentagram, representing the five elements and the unity of all things, is a central symbol in Wiccan practice. Other symbols, such as the triple moon, ankh, spiral, pentacle, triquetra, athame, wand, chalice, cauldron, and besom, each carry unique meanings and applications, enriching practitioners' spiritual and magical experiences. By understanding and working with these symbols, Wiccans can deepen their connection with the divine, harness the energies of the elements, and navigate the cycles and patterns that shape their spiritual journey.

CHAPTER IV

Rituals and Spells

The Structure of a Wiccan Ritual

Wicca, a modern pagan religious movement, encompasses a rich tapestry of rituals and ceremonies designed to connect practitioners with the divine, nature, and their inner selves. The structure of a Wiccan ritual is both art and discipline, combining ancient traditions with personal creativity. This section will explore the detailed steps to creating and performing a Wiccan ritual, emphasizing casting the circle and calling the quarters, two foundational practices in the Wiccan ceremony.

Creating and performing a Wiccan ritual involves several preparatory steps before the ceremony begins. The process starts with setting a clear intention. Intentions are the heart of any ritual, serving as the guiding purpose that shapes every action and element within the ceremony. Whether the intention is for healing, protection, celebration, or thanksgiving, the practitioner must clearly define and deeply understand it. This clarity ensures that all the energies and efforts are aligned towards a singular goal.

Once the intention is set, the next step is to gather the necessary tools and materials. Typical tools in a Wiccan ritual include the athame (a ritual knife), wand, chalice, pentacle, candles, incense, and offerings such as herbs or flowers. Each tool has symbolic meaning and practical use, contributing to the ritual's overall purpose. For instance, the athame is often used to direct energy and cast the circle, while the chalice represents the element of Water and is used in libations or symbolic offerings. Selecting the appropriate materials, including candles of specific colors, incense of certain scents, and herbs with particular properties, further enhances the ritual's effectiveness.

Selecting the right time and place for the ritual is also crucial. Many Wiccans follow the lunar calendar, choosing to perform rituals on the new moon, full moon, or other significant lunar phases. Sabbats mark the Wheel of the Year and are also expected ritual times. The location should be a quiet, undisturbed indoor or outdoor space that allows for a sense of privacy and connection with nature. Preparing the space involves cleaning it physically and energetically, often using methods like sweeping with a besom (ritual broom) or smudging with sage to clear away negative energies.

Before the ritual begins, practitioners often engage in personal purification. This can involve a ritual bath with salts and herbs to cleanse the body and mind or simple meditation to center and ground oneself. This step helps to separate the mundane from the sacred, allowing the practitioner to enter the ritual space with a clear and focused mind.

The ritual begins with casting the circle, creating a sacred and protected space for the ceremony. The circle acts as a boundary between the physical and spiritual realms, providing a safe space for energy work and communication with the divine. To cast the circle, the practitioner typically starts in the East and moves clockwise (deosil), using the athame or wand to trace the circle's boundary. Walking, they visualize a sphere of energy forming around them, protecting and containing the ritual space.

Once the circle is cast, the next step is to call the quarters, also known as the elements or elemental quarters. This practice involves invoking the presence and assistance of the four elements: Earth, Air, Fire, and Water, each associated with a cardinal direction. The East corresponds to Air, symbolizing intellect, communication, and beginnings. The South corresponds to Fire, representing passion, transformation, and energy. The West corresponds to Water, embodying emotions, intuition, and healing. The North corresponds to Earth, signifying stability, grounding, and materiality.

Calling the quarters is usually done clockwise, starting with the East. The practitioner stands facing their calling direction, raises their athame, wand, or hand, and recites an invocation specific to that element. For example, when calling Air in the East, they might say: "Hail, Guardians of the Watchtowers of the East, Powers of Air. I call upon you to witness this rite and guard this circle." They repeat this process for the South, West, and North, invoking the corresponding elemental guardians each time.

With the circle cast and the quarters called, the ritual space is now fully prepared, and the main body of the ritual can commence. This central part of the ritual varies widely depending on the purpose and intention set earlier. It may involve spellwork, meditation, chanting, dancing, or the enactment of symbolic actions. For instance, in a healing ritual, the practitioner might focus on visualizing the person in need enveloped in healing light, perhaps using a poppet or other symbolic representation to aid their focus. In a celebration ritual, such as a Sabbat, the practitioner might enact stories or myths related to the season, offering thanks and making offerings to the deities.

During this central part of the ritual, energy is often raised through various means such as chanting, drumming, dancing, or simply through focused intention and visualization. Increasing energy is to gather a powerful force that can be directed toward the ritual's intention. This energy is then released in a focused way, sending it out to manifest the desired outcome.

After the main work of the ritual is completed, the next step is to give thanks and make offerings. This is a crucial part of the ritual, acknowledging the assistance and presence of the divine, the elements, and any other spiritual entities that have been called upon. Offerings can be as simple as pouring a libation of Water or wine into the earth or leaving food, herbs, or other gifts in a designated place. Giving thanks helps maintain a balanced relationship with the spiritual forces and reinforces the practitioner's gratitude and respect.

The ritual concludes with the closing of the circle and the dismissal of the quarters. This is done counterclockwise (widdershins), starting with the North and moving to the West, South, and East. The practitioner stands facing each direction, raises their athame, wand, or hand, and recites a dismissal for the elemental guardians. For example, when dismissing Earth in the North, they might say: "Hail and farewell, Guardians of the Watchtowers of the North, Powers of Earth. Thank you for your presence and protection. Go if you must, stay if you will, but always remain in perfect love and trust." This process is repeated for the West, South, and East.

After dismissing the quarters, the practitioner formally opens the circle, again using their athame or wand to trace the boundary in a counterclockwise direction. As they walk, they visualize the sphere of energy dissolving and returning to the earth, thanking it for its protection and support. The formal opening of the circle marks the end of the ritual, and the practitioner can then ground themselves, often by eating and drinking something to help bring their awareness back to the physical world.

The structure of a Wiccan ritual, from preparation and casting the circle to calling the quarters, performing the central work, and closing the ritual, is a process rich with symbolic meaning and spiritual significance. Each step is designed to create a sacred space, focus the practitioner's intent, and connect with the divine and natural forces.

Beyond the specific steps, Wiccan rituals are characterized by their adaptability and personal expression. While traditional elements and practices exist, individual practitioners and covens often adapt rituals to suit their beliefs, preferences, and circumstances. This flexibility allows Wicca to be a profoundly personal and dynamic spiritual path, evolving with the needs and insights of its adherents.

Casting the circle and calling the quarters, in particular, exemplifies the Wiccan ritual's balance between structure and creativity. These practices establish a sacred space and invoke powerful elemental forces, creating a framework for practitioners to explore their spirituality and perform their magical work. At the same time, the words, gestures, and specific invocations used can vary widely, reflecting the unique perspectives and experiences of the practitioner.

The circle, as a sacred boundary, serves multiple functions. It protects the practitioner from external negative influences, contains and concentrates the energy raised within it, and creates a liminal space where the veil between the physical and spiritual worlds is thinned. This allows for a deeper connection with the divine, heightened intuition, and more effective magical work. Casting the circle is physical and spiritual, requiring focus, intention, and a clear visualization of the energy being directed.

Calling the quarters, meanwhile, brings in the energies of the four elements, each with its qualities and associations. This enhances the ritual's power and ensures that a balanced and holistic approach is taken. By acknowledging and inviting the presence of Earth, Air, Fire, and Water, the practitioner aligns themselves with the natural world and its cycles, fostering a more profound sense of connection and harmony.

The central work of the ritual, whether it involves spellwork, meditation, or celebration, is where the practitioner's intention is most directly expressed and enacted. This part of the ritual is highly varied and personal, reflecting the diversity of Wiccan practice. The methods used to raise and direct energy, the specific actions performed, and the symbols and tools employed all contribute to the overall effectiveness of the ritual. The practitioner's focus, intention, and emotional engagement are crucial at this stage, as these elements drive the magical work and bring about the desired change.

Giving thanks and making offerings after the central work reinforces the reciprocal nature of Wiccan spirituality. It acknowledges the interconnectedness of all things and the importance of maintaining a respectful and grateful relationship with the divine and the natural world. Offerings can take many forms, from simple gestures of gratitude to elaborate gifts, but their purpose is always to honor and thank the spiritual forces that have been invoked.

The circle's closing and the quarters' dismissal mark the transition back to the mundane world. These steps ensure that the sacred space is respectfully dissolved and that the energies and entities called upon are appropriately thanked and released. This helps maintain the integrity of the ritual space and the practitioner's spiritual practice, preventing residual energies from lingering and ensuring that the practitioner is grounded and centered.

The entire process of creating and performing a Wiccan ritual is a deeply immersive and transformative experience. It requires preparation, focus, and a deep understanding of the symbols and practices involved. At the same time, it allows for personal expression and creativity, enabling practitioners to tailor their rituals to their needs and circumstances. This balance between tradition and innovation is one of the strengths of Wiccan practice, allowing it to remain relevant and meaningful in a rapidly changing world.

In conclusion, the structure of a Wiccan ritual involves a series of carefully crafted steps, each imbued with symbolic meaning and spiritual significance. From setting the intention and gathering the tools to casting the circle, calling the quarters, performing the central work, giving thanks, and closing the ritual, each stage is designed to create a sacred space, focus the practitioner's intent, and connect with the divine and natural forces. The practices of casting the circle and calling the quarters are foundational elements that establish the ritual framework, bringing protection, balance, and powerful elemental energies into the ceremony. By engaging in these practices, Wiccans can deepen their connection with the divine, enhance their magical work, and foster greater harmony and balance. The adaptability and personal expression inherent in Wiccan rituals ensure that this spiritual path remains dynamic, relevant, and deeply fulfilling for those who walk it.

Crafting Effective Spells

Spellwork is a fundamental aspect of Wiccan and many other magical traditions, involving the deliberate use of intention, symbols, and actions to bring about a desired change or outcome. Crafting effective spells requires understanding the basic principles of magic, writing and personalizing spells, and the importance of various components such as timing, tools, and correspondences. This section thoroughly explores these aspects, providing a comprehensive guide to effective spellcraft.

The foundation of any spell is intention. Intention is the clear, focused purpose behind the spell and the driving force that channels the practitioner's energy towards achieving the desired result. Before crafting a spell, it is essential to have a precise and well-defined intention. This clarity helps to focus the mind and ensures that all the spell elements are aligned with the goal. Vague or conflicting intentions can dilute the spell's effectiveness, making it harder to achieve the desired outcome.

Once the intention is set, the next step is to choose the appropriate timing for the spell. Timing can significantly influence the spell's potency, and many practitioners align their spells with lunar phases, days of the week, and specific times of day. For example, the waxing moon phase is ideal for spells related to growth, attraction, and new beginnings, while the waning moon phase is suited for banishing, releasing, and letting go. Each day of the week is associated with particular planetary influences and can enhance certain spells. For instance, Sunday is linked to the sun and is favorable for success, prosperity, and health, while Friday, associated with Venus, is ideal for love and beauty spells.

The next step in crafting a spell is to gather the necessary tools and materials. These can include candles, herbs, crystals, incense, oils, and other items corresponding to the spell's intention. Each tool and material carries its energy and symbolism, which can amplify the spell's power. For instance, a green candle might be used in a prosperity spell due to its association with growth and abundance. At the same time, rose quartz might be chosen for a love spell because of its connection to emotional healing and romantic energy. Understanding these correspondences and selecting materials that align with the spell's intention is crucial for effective spellcraft.

Writing the spell is a critical part of the process, as it involves articulating the intention and the specific actions to be taken. A well-written spell includes a clear statement of intent, often called magic or affirmation, which expresses the desired outcome in positive, present-tense language. For example, instead of saying, "I want to find love," a more effective magic would be, "I am surrounded by love and attract my perfect partner." This phrasing assumes that the desired outcome is already happening, which helps to create a sense of certainty and confidence in the practitioner.

In addition to the magic, the spell should outline the steps to be taken, including using tools and materials, any physical actions (such as lighting a candle or sprinkling herbs), and the timing of these actions. The sequence of steps should be logical and cohesive, creating a ritual that flows smoothly and builds energy towards the spell's culmination. Repetition of key phrases or actions can also help to develop and direct energy, reinforcing the spell's intention.

Personalizing a spell is another crucial aspect of effective spellcraft. While many traditional spells are available in books and online, personalizing a spell to suit one's needs and circumstances can significantly enhance its effectiveness. Personalization can involve tailoring the magic to reflect the practitioner's unique voice and style, choosing materials with personal significance, and incorporating individual symbols or gestures. This customization helps to create a stronger emotional and energetic connection to the spell, making it more powerful and effective.

One way to personalize a spell is to include personal items, such as photographs, pieces of clothing, or objects that have been charged with personal energy. These items can directly link the practitioner and the spell's intention, amplifying the connection and focus. For example, in a spell for protection, a personal item like a piece of jewelry can be charged with protective energy and worn as a talisman.

Visualization is another critical component of effective spellcraft. Visualization involves creating a mental image of the desired outcome, which helps to focus the practitioner's mind and direct their energy towards the goal. During the spell, the practitioner should visualize the outcome as vividly and clearly as possible, engaging all their senses to make the image real and tangible. This mental rehearsal helps to imprint the intention on the subconscious mind and the universal energy, increasing the likelihood of manifestation.

Casting the spell involves performing the steps outlined in the written spell, including any physical actions, recitations, and visualizations. This is when the practitioner channels their energy and intention into the spell, often entering a meditative or trance-like state to enhance their focus and connection. Rhythmic actions, such as chanting, drumming, or dancing, can help raise and direct energy, creating a powerful and dynamic flow that supports the spell's intention.

Grounding and centering are essential practices both before and after casting a spell. Grounding helps to connect the practitioner with the Earth's energy, providing stability and balance, while centering helps to focus the mind and align the practitioner's energy with their intention. Techniques for grounding can include walking barefoot on the Earth, holding a grounding stone like a hematite, or visualizing roots growing from the body into the ground. Centering can involve deep breathing, meditation, or visualizing a light point within the body representing the practitioner's essence.

After the spell is cast, it is essential to release attachment to the outcome and trust that the energy has been set in motion. This detachment helps to prevent anxiety and doubt from undermining the spell's effectiveness. Practitioners are encouraged to focus on positive actions and attitudes that support the desired outcome while also being open to unexpected ways in which the intention might manifest.

In addition to these basic principles, several advanced techniques and considerations can further enhance the effectiveness of spellcraft. One such technique is using sigils, symbols created to represent a specific intention or desire. Sigils are often used instead of written words or chants, providing a visual focus for the spell. Creating a sigil involves reducing the intention to a simple, unique symbol, which is then charged with energy through visualization, repetition, or other methods. Once the sigil is charged, it can be incorporated into the spell or placed in a prominent location as a reminder of the intention.

Another advanced technique is using planetary correspondences, which involves aligning the spell with the energies of specific planets. Each planet is associated with certain qualities and influences, which can enhance different types of spells. For example, Venus is associated with love, beauty, and harmony, making it ideal for love spells. At the same time, Mars is linked to courage, strength, and protection, suitable for spells involving assertiveness or defense. Understanding these correspondences and timing the spell to coincide with the appropriate planetary influences can add more potency to the work.

Astrological considerations, such as the positions of the sun, moon, and planets, can also play a significant role in spellcraft. Many practitioners consult astrological charts to determine the best times for casting spells, considering factors such as lunar phases, planetary transits, and aspects. This alignment with cosmic energies can enhance the spell's effectiveness and ensure that the practitioner is working in harmony with the natural flow of the universe.

Incorporating the elements – Earth, Air, Fire, and Water – is another powerful way to enhance spellwork. Each component has its qualities and correspondences and can be invoked to support different aspects of the spell. Earth represents stability, grounding, and material manifestation, making it suitable for spells involving prosperity, health, and protection. Air symbolizes intellect, communication, and new beginnings, ideal for spells related to knowledge, travel, and inspiration. Fire embodies passion, transformation, and energy, perfect for spells involving courage, creativity, and purification. Water signifies emotions, intuition, and healing, making it appropriate for spells related to love, empathy, and psychic abilities. By incorporating the elements into spellcraft, practitioners can draw on the full spectrum of natural energies to support their work.

An essential aspect of effective spellcraft is ethical consideration. Practitioners are encouraged to adhere to the Wiccan Rede, which states, "An it harm none, do what ye will." This principle emphasizes the importance of avoiding harm to oneself and others and encourages practitioners to consider the potential consequences of their actions. Ethical spellcraft involves using one's power responsibly and with respect for the free will and well-being of others. This consideration not only aligns with the moral values of many practitioners but also helps to ensure that the spell's energy is positive and constructive.

Record-keeping is another valuable practice in spellcraft. Maintaining a journal or Book of Shadows to document spells, their components, and outcomes can provide useful insights and help practitioners refine their techniques. By recording the details of each spell, including the intention, timing, tools, steps, and results, practitioners can track their progress, identify patterns, and learn from their experiences. This practice also helps to preserve personal knowledge and traditions, creating a rich resource for future work.

Finally, reflection and evaluation are crucial components of effective spellcraft. After casting a spell, it is essential to reflect on the experience, considering what went well, what could be improved, and what insights were gained. This reflection can help practitioners to develop their skills, deepen their understanding, and enhance the effectiveness of their spells. Evaluation also involves assessing the outcomes of the spell, observing how the intention manifested, and any changes that occurred. This feedback loop helps to refine the practitioner's techniques and ensure that their spellwork continues to evolve and improve.

In conclusion, crafting effective spells involves a combination of clear intention, appropriate timing, using tools and correspondences, careful writing, and personalization. Understanding the basic principles of spellcraft, such as the importance of intention, visualization, and ethical consideration, provides a solid foundation for successful work. Advanced techniques, including using sigils, planetary correspondences, and elemental energies, can further enhance the potency of spells. Record-keeping, reflection, and evaluation are valuable practices that support continuous learning and improvement. By integrating these elements into their spellcraft, practitioners can harness the power of magic to create positive change and manifest their desires in alignment with their highest good.

Ethics and Responsibility in Magic

In its many forms and traditions, magic holds a profound allure for those who seek to understand and manipulate the forces of nature and the unseen world. However, with the power to influence and change comes significant ethical responsibility. Magic practitioners must navigate a complex moral and ethical considerations landscape to ensure their actions do not harm others, violate free will, or disrupt the natural order. This section explores the ethical implications of magical practice, emphasizing the importance of respecting free will and adhering to natural laws.

The foundation of ethical magical practice lies in the principle of "harm none." This concept, deeply rooted in many mystical traditions, particularly Wicca, is a guiding precept for responsible magic. The Wiccan Rede, a critical ethical statement in Wicca, famously articulates this principle: "An it harm none, do what ye will." This tenet underscores the importance of ensuring that one's magical actions do not cause harm to oneself, others, or the environment. The notion of harm extends beyond physical injury to include emotional, mental, and spiritual harm, emphasizing a holistic approach to ethical practice.

Respecting free will is another cornerstone of ethical magical practice. Free will is the inherent right of individuals to make their own choices and decisions without undue influence or coercion. In the context of magic, this means that practitioners should avoid spells or actions that seek to control, manipulate, or infringe upon the autonomy of others. For example, love spells aimed at a specific person are often considered unethical because they attempt to override the individual's free will and compel them to feel or act in a certain way. Instead, ethical practitioners might opt for spells that generally attract love, allowing the universe to bring a compatible partner naturally.

Understanding and respecting natural laws is also crucial for ethical magical practice. In this context, natural laws refer to the fundamental principles governing the physical and metaphysical worlds. These include the laws of cause and effect, the principle of balance, and the interconnectedness of all things. Magic operates within these natural laws, and attempting to contravene them can lead to unintended and often harmful consequences. For example, a practitioner who seeks to gain wealth through magical means must be aware that such an action could disrupt the natural flow of resources and energies, potentially causing imbalance. Ethical practitioners strive to work in harmony with these natural laws, using magic to enhance and support the natural order rather than disrupt it.

One of the significant ethical challenges in magical practice is the issue of intent versus impact. A practitioner's intentions might be positive, but the effect of their actions can still be harmful. For instance, a spell intended to protect a loved one might inadvertently create a barrier that isolates them from beneficial experiences or relationships. Ethical practice requires ongoing self-reflection and a willingness to consider the broader implications of one's actions. Practitioners must continually assess and reassess their motives, methods, and the potential outcomes of their spells and rituals.

Another important aspect of ethical magical practice is accountability. Practitioners must take responsibility for the outcomes of their actions, whether intentional or unintended. This means acknowledging mistakes, learning from them, and making amends where possible. In some traditions, this concept is formalized through karma or the Threefold Law, which posits that the energy one puts into the world, whether positive or negative, will return to them threefold. This principle encourages practitioners to act with integrity and mindfulness, understanding that their actions have far-reaching consequences.

Cultural sensitivity and respect are also critical components of ethical magical practice. Many mystical traditions and practices are rooted in specific cultural contexts, and appropriating these practices with proper understanding and respect can be beneficial and respectful. Ethical practitioners try to educate themselves about the origins and cultural significance of the practices they engage in, seeking to honor and preserve the integrity of those traditions. This might involve seeking permission from cultural gatekeepers, crediting the sources, and avoiding the commercialization or trivialization of sacred practices.

The use of magical tools and ingredients also carries ethical considerations. Practitioners should be mindful of the sources of their materials, ensuring that they are obtained sustainably and respectfully. This includes avoiding the exploitation of natural resources, respecting the rights of indigenous communities, and being aware of the environmental impact of their practices. For example, overharvesting certain herbs or crystals can lead to ecological damage and depletion of these resources. Ethical practitioners strive to use ethically sourced, renewable, and environmentally friendly materials.

Confidentiality and consent are crucial when performing magic on behalf of others. Practitioners should always obtain explicit permission from the person for whom they are casting a spell or performing a ritual. Performing magic without consent violates personal boundaries and can be considered energetic coercion. Additionally, practitioners must respect the privacy and confidentiality of those they work with, maintaining discretion and integrity in their magical practices.

The practitioner's role as a guide or teacher also involves ethical responsibilities. Those who teach or lead others in magical practice must do so with honesty, humility, and respect for their students' autonomy and individual paths. Ethical teachers provide accurate information, encourage critical thinking, and support their students' growth and development without imposing their beliefs or agendas. They acknowledge the limits of their knowledge and are open to learning from others, fostering a culture of mutual respect and shared learning.

Ethical magical practice also involves a commitment to personal and spiritual growth. Practitioners are encouraged to engage in regular self-reflection, meditation, and study to deepen their understanding of themselves, their practice, and the world around them. This ongoing process of self-improvement helps to cultivate the virtues of humility, compassion, and wisdom, which are essential for ethical practice. By striving to become better versions of themselves, practitioners can ensure their magic is used for the highest good and aligned with moral principles.

The concept of reciprocity is another key ethical consideration in magic. Reciprocity involves recognizing and honoring the interconnectedness of all things and understanding that the energy and resources one receives must be balanced by giving back in some way. This can take the form of offering gratitude and respect to the natural world, contributing to the well-being of one's community, or performing acts of service and kindness. Ethical practitioners are mindful of maintaining balance and harmony in their interactions with the world, using their magical abilities to contribute positively to the whole.

In addition to individual ethical considerations, magical communities also play a role in promoting ethical practice. Communities can establish codes of conduct, provide education and support, and hold members accountable for their actions. By fostering a culture of ethical awareness and mutual respect, magical communities can help practitioners navigate the complex moral landscape and ensure their practices align with shared values and principles.

Ethical magical practice also involves a commitment to truth and authenticity. Practitioners should strive to be honest with themselves and others about their abilities, experiences, and intentions. This includes avoiding deception, exaggeration, or misrepresenting one's skills or achievements. Authenticity requires a willingness to confront one's limitations and challenges and approach magical practice with humility and openness. By being truthful and genuine, practitioners can build trust and integrity in their relationships and communities.

Another important aspect of ethical magical practice is considering the broader societal and environmental impact of one's actions. Magic does not exist in a vacuum; it is interconnected with the world's physical, social, and ecological systems. Ethical practitioners are mindful of the potential ripple effects of their actions and strive to use their abilities to promote social justice, environmental sustainability, and the well-being of all beings. This might involve using magic to support causes such as conservation, human rights, and community healing or simply being conscious of how one's practices affect the more extensive web of life.

Ethical dilemmas are inevitable in magical practice, and practitioners must be prepared to navigate these challenges with wisdom and integrity. This requires a deep understanding of one's values, a willingness to seek guidance and counsel, and the ability to make difficult decisions aligned with ethical principles. Ethical dilemmas often involve complex situations with no clear right or wrong answers, and practitioners must rely on their inner moral compass, intuition, and the guidance of trusted mentors and peers to find the best course of action.

In some cases, ethical practice may require restraint and discernment. Not all desires or impulses should be acted upon magically, and practitioners must be able to distinguish between what is beneficial and what might be harmful or unnecessary. This discernment involves carefully considering one's motives, the potential consequences, and the alignment of the action with one's higher self and ethical values. By exercising restraint and making thoughtful, deliberate choices, practitioners can ensure that their magic serves the greater good and aligns with their moral commitments.

Exploring ethics and responsibility in magic also involves understanding the historical and cultural contexts in which magical practices have developed. Many mystical traditions have their roots in ancient cultures and have evolved in response to changing social, political, and environmental conditions. Ethical practitioners are mindful of this history and seek to honor and preserve the wisdom and knowledge of past generations. This includes knowing how magic has been used positively and negatively throughout history and learning from these experiences to guide current and future practice.

The relationship between magic and science is another important consideration in ethical practice. While magic and science are often seen as distinct or opposing fields, they both seek to understand and influence the world meaningfully. Ethical practitioners respect the contributions of science and are open to integrating scientific knowledge and methods into their practice. This might involve using scientific principles to enhance the effectiveness of spells, respecting the findings of environmental science in the sourcing of materials, or being open to collaboration with scientific communities to explore the intersections between magic and science.

Ethical magical practice also involves a commitment to ongoing learning and development. The field of magic is vast and ever-evolving, and practitioners must be willing to engage in continuous study and exploration. This includes staying informed about new developments, deepening one's understanding of traditional knowledge, and being open to new perspectives and approaches. By embracing a mindset of lifelong learning, practitioners can ensure that their practice remains dynamic, relevant, and aligned with ethical principles.

In conclusion, ethics and responsibility in magic are fundamental aspects that underpin the practice of magic in all its forms. Understanding the ethical implications of magical actions, respecting free will, and adhering to natural laws are essential for ensuring that magic is used positively, constructively, and responsibly. Ethical practice involves a commitment to harm none, respect for free will, accountability, cultural sensitivity, and a deep understanding of natural laws. Practitioners must navigate the complex landscape of ethical considerations with wisdom, integrity, and humility, continuously reflecting on their actions and their impact on the world. By adhering to these moral principles, practitioners can harness the power of magic to create positive change, promote harmony, and contribute to the greater good. The ongoing journey of ethical magical practice is one of self-discovery, growth, and profound connection with the natural and spiritual worlds, guiding practitioners to use their abilities in ways that honor the interconnectedness of all life and the fundamental principles of respect and responsibility.

CHAPTER V

Deities and Spiritual Beings

The Wiccan Concept of Deity

Wicca, a modern pagan religious movement, emphasizes the worship of nature and the divine in various forms. Central to Wiccan belief is the concept of deity, which is often expressed through the archetypes of the God and Goddess. These deities symbolize the duality and unity inherent in the divine, reflecting a balance of masculine and feminine energies. This section explores the Wiccan understanding of deity, focusing on the God and Goddess and how their duality and unity form a cohesive spiritual worldview.

The Wiccan concept of deity is rooted in the belief that the divine is immanent in the natural world and within all living beings. This pantheistic view asserts that the sacred permeates everything, from the smallest particle to the vast cosmos. In Wicca, the divine is typically personified through the God and Goddess, representing the male and female aspects of the universal life force. These deities are not seen as separate, distant entities but as integral parts of the same divine source, reflecting the interconnectedness of all existence.

The Goddess, often called the Great Mother, embodies the feminine principle in Wiccan theology. She is associated with the Earth, fertility, creation, and the nurturing aspects of nature. The Goddess is often depicted in three forms, corresponding to the phases of the Moon: the Maiden, the Mother, and the Crone. The Maiden symbolizes youth, new beginnings, and the waxing Moon; the Mother represents maturity, fertility, and the full Moon; and the Crone signifies wisdom, transformation, and the waning Moon. These aspects illustrate the cyclical nature of life and the continuous process of birth, growth, death, and rebirth.

On the other hand, God represents the masculine principle and is often associated with the Sun, the hunt, and the wild aspects of nature. He is commonly depicted as the Horned God, a figure that combines elements of the stag and the goat, symbolizing strength, virility, and the primal forces of nature. God is also seen as a consort to the Goddess, and their relationship is central to the Wiccan understanding of the divine. Together, they represent the balance of opposites—light and dark, life and death, male and female—and the dynamic interplay of these forces that sustains the universe.

In Wicca, the God and Goddess are celebrated through the Wheel of the Year, a cycle of eight seasonal festivals known as Sabbats. These festivals mark critical points in the agricultural and solar cycles, reflecting the changing relationship between the deities and the natural world. For example, at Beltane, the God and Goddess are honored as lovers, symbolizing the fertility and vitality of spring. At Samhain, the God is seen as the dying and reborn deity, reflecting the cycle of death and rebirth inherent in nature. These rituals emphasize the interconnectedness of life and the continuous flow of energy between the divine and the mundane.

The duality of the God and Goddess in Wiccan belief highlights the complementary nature of masculine and feminine energies. This duality is not viewed as a dichotomy but as a harmonious balance, where both aspects are equally valued and essential for the wholeness of the divine. The interplay of these energies is seen in the natural world, where opposites such as day and night, summer and winter, and growth and decay coexist in a dynamic equilibrium. This balance is also reflected in the human experience, where individuals embody masculine and feminine qualities regardless of gender.

While the God and Goddess represent distinct aspects of the divine, Wiccan theology emphasizes their unity. The concept of the sacred as a singular, unified source is often expressed through the term "the One" or "the All." This notion suggests that the God and Goddess are manifestations of a more excellent, ineffable divine essence that transcends duality. In this sense, the Wiccan understanding of deity encompasses the diversity and unity of the holy, acknowledging the diverse expressions of the sacred while recognizing their underlying oneness.

The unity of the God and Goddess is symbolized in various Wiccan rituals and practices. One such symbol is the pentacle, a five-pointed star enclosed within a circle. The points of the star represent the four elements—Earth, Air, Fire, and Water—plus Spirit, which unifies them. The circle signifies the wholeness and interconnectedness of all things, emphasizing the unity of the divine. Similarly, the ritual of Drawing Down the Moon involves invoking the Goddess into the High Priestess, while Drawing Down the Sun invokes the God into the High Priest. These rituals underscore the immanence of the divine in human beings and the sacred marriage of the God and Goddess within each individual.

Wiccan practices also emphasize personal experience and direct communion with the divine. Meditation, visualization, and ritual are tools used to connect with the God and Goddess and to attune to their energies. These practices foster a reverence for nature and life cycles, encouraging practitioners to live harmoniously with the world around them. The Wiccan Rede, "An it harm none, do what ye will," encapsulates the ethical framework of Wicca, emphasizing personal responsibility and the interconnectedness of all actions.

The Wiccan concept of deity also reflects a broader, more inclusive approach to spirituality. Wiccans often draw from various mythologies and cultural traditions, recognizing the many faces of the divine. The God and Goddess are archetypes, representing universal principles that transcend specific cultural and religious contexts. This inclusive perspective allows for a diverse and eclectic practice where individuals can find personal meaning and connection with the divine in ways that resonate with them.

In contemporary Wicca, there is also an increasing recognition of gender diversity and the fluidity of gender identities. The traditional binary of the God and Goddess is being re-examined to include non-binary, transgender, and genderqueer perspectives. This evolution reflects a broader understanding of the divine as encompassing all expressions of gender and sexuality and a commitment to inclusivity and equality within the Wiccan community.

The duality and unity of the divine in Wiccan belief offer a profound and holistic understanding of the sacred. The God and Goddess, as expressions of the masculine and feminine principles, represent the dynamic balance of opposites that sustains the universe. Their relationship illustrates the interconnectedness of all things and the continuous cycle of life, death, and rebirth. At the same time, the unity of the divine emphasizes the oneness of all creation, transcending duality and celebrating the diversity of the sacred.

In conclusion, the Wiccan concept of deity, embodied in the God and Goddess, provides a rich and nuanced framework for understanding the divine. The duality and unity of these deities reflect the balance of masculine and feminine energies, the interconnectedness of all existence, and the continuous flow of life. Through rituals, practices, and an inclusive approach to spirituality, Wiccans honor the sacred in its many forms, fostering a deep connection with the natural world and the divine within. This holistic perspective offers a path of spiritual growth and harmony, encouraging individuals to live in alignment with the rhythms of nature and the universal life force.

Working with Deities

Working with deities and building relationships with specific divine beings is integral to many spiritual traditions. This practice involves recognizing and honoring the presence of these deities, understanding their unique characteristics and influences, and fostering a personal connection with them through various rituals, offerings, and prayers. This section explores the multifaceted nature of working with deities, focusing on building relationships with specific deities and the importance of offerings and prayers in this spiritual endeavor.

In many polytheistic and pagan traditions, deities are seen as distinct, individual beings with their personalities, domains, and attributes. Unlike monotheistic religions that worship a single, all-encompassing deity, polytheistic traditions recognize a pantheon of gods and goddesses, each overseeing different aspects of life and the cosmos. Building relationships with these deities involves identifying which ones resonate with an individual's spiritual path, needs, and personal characteristics.

Identifying a specific deity to work with often begins with research and exploration. This can involve reading myths, studying historical texts, and learning about the cultural contexts in which these deities were worshipped initially. Many people feel drawn to specific deities through an intuitive sense of connection, dreams, or synchronicities. Others may seek the guidance of more experienced practitioners, such as priests, priestesses, or spiritual mentors, who can provide insights and recommendations based on their experiences and knowledge.

Once a specific deity is identified, the next step is establishing a connection. This often involves setting up a sacred space or altar dedicated to the deity. An altar is a focal point for worship and can include images or statues of the deity, symbols associated with them, candles, incense, and other items that hold spiritual significance. Creating this sacred space is an act of devotion and respect, signaling to the deity that they are welcome in the practitioner's life.

Offerings are a crucial aspect of building a relationship with a deity. In many traditions, offerings are seen as gifts or tokens of appreciation to honor the god and seek their favor or guidance. The nature of the offerings can vary widely depending on the deity and the tradition. Standard offerings include food and drink, flowers, herbs, crystals, and items of personal significance. For example, a practitioner working with a goddess associated with fertility might offer fruits, grains, and honey, while someone seeking the protection of a warrior god might offer weapons or objects symbolizing strength and courage.

Making an offering is more than just a material transaction; it is a profoundly spiritual act that fosters a reciprocal relationship between the practitioner and the deity. It expresses gratitude, respect, and recognition of the deity's presence and influence. Offerings can be made regularly, such as daily or weekly, or on special occasions and festivals associated with the deity. They can also be made in times of need to seek the deity's assistance or intervention in specific situations.

Prayers and invocations are another vital component of working with deities. Through prayer, practitioners communicate their thoughts, feelings, desires, and intentions to the deity. Prayers can be formal or informal, spoken aloud or silently, and include traditional invocations, chants, hymns, or spontaneous expressions of devotion. The purpose of prayer is to seek assistance or blessings and cultivate a deeper understanding and connection with the deity.

In many traditions, specific prayers and invocations are associated with particular deities. These prayers often include the deity's names, epithets, and attributes and may recount their myths and deeds. Reciting these prayers helps to invoke the deity's presence and align the practitioner with their energy and influence. It is expected to incorporate meditative practices, such as visualization and contemplation, to deepen the connection and open oneself to the deity's guidance and wisdom.

Building a relationship with a deity is a dynamic and evolving process. It requires time, patience, and dedication. As with any relationship, listening, observing, and being receptive to the deity's messages and signs is essential. These can come in various forms: dreams, intuitive insights, synchronicities, and even physical sensations. Paying attention to these signs and reflecting on their meanings can provide valuable insights and strengthen the bond with the deity.

In addition to offerings and prayers, rituals and ceremonies play a significant role in honoring and working with deities. These rituals can vary widely depending on the tradition and the honored deity. They often involve a combination of elements, such as music, dance, chanting, invocations, and sacred objects and symbols. Rituals create a holy space and time, allowing practitioners to step outside the mundane world and enter a liminal state to connect more deeply with the divine.

One common type of ritual is the seasonal or cyclical celebration, such as the festivals marking the turning of the Wheel of the Year in pagan traditions. These festivals honor the changing seasons and the corresponding aspects of the associated deities. For example, Samhain, celebrated at the end of October, honors the ancestors and the deities associated with death and the underworld, while Beltane, celebrated in May, honors the deities of fertility and the blossoming of life.

Another critical aspect of working with deities is the concept of personal gnosis or direct spiritual knowledge. While traditional texts and established rituals provide a foundation, personal gnosis allows practitioners to develop unique relationships and understandings of the deities. This can involve receiving personal messages, visions, or guidance from the deity and incorporating these experiences into one's spiritual practice. Personal gnosis emphasizes spirituality's experiential and individualized nature, allowing for a more intimate and personal connection with the divine.

It is also essential to approach the relationship with humility and respect. Deities are potent beings with agency and will, and it is important to honor their boundaries and wishes. This includes being mindful of cultural appropriation and respecting the traditions and practices associated with the deity's original cultural context. Working with deities from cultures different from one's own requires sensitivity, research, and a commitment to honoring the integrity and significance of those traditions.

Working with deities is not limited to individual worship; it often extends to community and collective rituals. Many spiritual traditions have communal ceremonies, where practitioners unite to honor the deities, share offerings, and participate in rituals. These gatherings foster a sense of community and shared spiritual purpose, reinforcing the connection between the practitioners and the deities. They also provide an opportunity for collective energy and intention to be focused on a common goal, amplifying the power and impact of the ritual.

In some traditions, practitioners may be called to serve as priests or priestesses, acting as intermediaries between the community and the deities. These roles often involve extensive training, initiation, and a deep commitment to the deity and the spiritual path. Priests and priestesses perform rituals, offer guidance and support to the community, and maintain the sacred spaces and altars dedicated to the deities. They facilitate the connection between the deities and the community, ensuring the rituals and practices are carried out with reverence and integrity.

The relationships that practitioners build with deities can profoundly impact their lives. These relationships provide guidance, inspiration, and support, helping individuals navigate the challenges and uncertainties of life. The presence of the deity can offer comfort and reassurance, reminding practitioners that they are not alone and that a greater spiritual force supports them. This sense of connection and support can be essential in times of crisis or transition, providing a source of strength and resilience.

Furthermore, working with deities can foster personal growth and transformation. Building a relationship with a deity often involves confronting one's limitations, fears, and insecurities. The deity's guidance and influence can help practitioners overcome these challenges, encouraging them to develop their strengths and realize their potential. This transformative process is reflected in the archetypal journeys and myths associated with many deities, where the hero or heroine undergoes trials and challenges, ultimately emerging stronger and wiser.

In conclusion, working with deities and building relationships with specific divine beings is a rich and multifaceted practice encompassing research, devotion, offerings, prayers, and rituals. It involves identifying deities that resonate with one's spiritual path, creating sacred spaces, and making offerings as acts of devotion and respect. Prayers and invocations facilitate communication with the deity, fostering a deeper connection and alignment with their energy. Rituals and ceremonies create sacred time and space, allowing for a profound connection with the divine. Personal gnosis and direct spiritual experiences further deepen the relationship, allowing for a unique and individualized connection with the deity. This practice requires humility, respect, and a commitment to honoring the deities and their traditions. Through these practices, practitioners can cultivate a profound and transformative relationship with the divine, drawing on the deities' guidance, support, and inspiration in their spiritual journey.

Spirits and Other Entities

Throughout human history, the belief in spirits and other entities has significantly shaped spiritual practices and worldviews. These entities, including nature spirits, elementals, ancestors, and guides, are often considered integral to the natural world and the spiritual realm. They serve as intermediaries between humans and the divine, providing guidance, protection, and wisdom. This section explores the various types of spirits and entities, focusing on their characteristics, roles, and how individuals and cultures interact with them.

Nature spirits are believed to inhabit natural features such as trees, rivers, mountains, and other landscapes. These spirits are often seen as the guardians and essence of the natural world, embodying its vitality and consciousness. Many cultures have myths and legends that describe interactions with nature spirits, often portraying them as powerful and capricious beings that demand respect and reverence. In some traditions, nature spirits are known as fairies, elves, or devas, each with unique characteristics and domains.

The relationship between humans and nature spirits is often reciprocal. Humans may offer gifts, prayers, and rituals to honor these spirits, seeking their favor and protection. In return, nature spirits are believed to bestow blessings, fertility, and harmony upon the land and its inhabitants. This relationship emphasizes the interconnectedness of all life and the importance of living in harmony with the natural world. Many indigenous cultures strongly connect with nature spirits, incorporating them into their daily lives and spiritual practices.

Elementals are a specific type of nature spirit associated with the classical elements of earth, air, fire, and water. Each elemental is believed to embody the essence and qualities of its respective element. For example, earth elementals, often called gnomes, are associated with stability, fertility, and material wealth. Air elementals, known as sylphs, are linked to intellect, communication, and freedom. Fire elementals, or salamanders, represent transformation, passion, and energy. Water elementals, called undines or nereids, are connected to emotions, intuition, and healing.

Working with elementals involves recognizing and honoring their presence in the natural world and within oneself. Elemental magic and rituals often seek to invoke the qualities of the elements and harmonize their energies. For example, a ritual to summon earth elementals might involve burying crystals or planting seeds, symbolizing a desire for stability and growth. Similarly, invoking water elementals might involve rituals near rivers or oceans, seeking emotional healing and clarity. The balance and harmony of the elements within and around us are essential for spiritual and physical well-being.

Ancestors play a central role in many spiritual traditions, linking the living and the spiritual realm. Ancestral spirits are believed to offer their descendants guidance, protection, and support. They are often honored through rituals, offerings, and remembrance, acknowledging their contributions and maintaining a connection with the past. Ancestor worship and veneration are particularly prominent in African, Asian, and indigenous cultures, where the continuity of family and community is deeply valued.

The practice of ancestor veneration involves creating altars or shrines dedicated to one's ancestors, often featuring photographs, heirlooms, and offerings of food, drink, and incense. These altars serve as focal points for communication and communion with the ancestors. Prayers and rituals may be performed to seek the ancestors' guidance, express gratitude, or request assistance. The belief in the continued presence and influence of the ancestors reinforces the idea of an unbroken lineage and the enduring connection between generations.

Spirit guides, also known as guardian spirits or totem animals, are believed to offer protection, wisdom, and support to individuals on their spiritual journeys. These guides are often seen as benevolent beings who help navigate life's challenges and provide insight into one's path and purpose. Spirit guides can take many forms, including animals, mythological creatures, and ancestral spirits. The concept of spirit guides is found in various spiritual traditions, including shamanism, Native American spirituality, and New Age practices.

Connecting with a spirit guide often involves meditation, visualization, and other spiritual practices designed to open one's awareness to the presence and messages of the guide. This relationship is highly personal and unique, with the guide offering tailored guidance and support based on the individual's needs and circumstances. Spirit guides are seen as allies on the spiritual journey, providing wisdom and encouragement and helping to align one's actions with their higher purpose.

In shamanic traditions, the shaman serves as an intermediary between the physical and spiritual realms, often working with various spirits and entities. Shamans undergo rigorous training and initiation to develop their abilities to communicate with spirits and perform healing rituals. They may journey to the spirit world through trance, drumming, or other altered states of consciousness, seeking guidance and assistance from spirit allies. The shaman's role is to restore balance and harmony within individuals and the community by addressing spiritual imbalances and facilitating healing.

Many spiritual traditions also recognize the existence of darker or evil spirits, often called demons, jinn, or evil spirits. These entities are believed to cause harm, illness, or misfortune and are usually associated with chaos, negativity, and spiritual corruption. Protective rituals and practices are employed to ward off these negative influences and maintain spiritual purity. This can include talismans, prayers, and rituals designed to banish or neutralize harmful entities.

There is a growing interest in working with spirits and other entities in modern spiritual practices as part of a holistic approach to spirituality and self-development. This includes exploring a variety of spiritual traditions and practices, often blending elements from different cultures and belief systems. For example, individuals might combine practices from shamanism, Wicca, and New Age spirituality to create a personalized spiritual path that resonates with their experiences and beliefs.

Working with spirits and entities requires a respectful and mindful approach. It is essential to recognize the autonomy and agency of these beings, treating them with reverence and gratitude. This includes awareness of cultural sensitivities and avoiding appropriation or misrepresenting spiritual practices and beliefs. Building a relationship with spirits and entities is a reciprocal process, requiring time, dedication, and a willingness to listen and learn.

The concept of spirits and entities also extends to the animistic worldview, where all things—living and non-living—are believed to possess a spirit or consciousness. This perspective emphasizes the interconnectedness and sacredness of all life, encouraging a deep respect for nature and the environment. Animism is a foundational belief in many indigenous cultures, where the natural world is seen as alive and imbued with spiritual significance.

In conclusion, believing in spirits and other entities encompasses many beings, including nature spirits, elementals, ancestors, and guides. These entities play vital roles in many spiritual traditions, serving as intermediaries between humans and the divine and offering guidance, protection, and wisdom. Working with these spirits involves a combination of rituals, offerings, prayers, and personal practices designed to honor their presence and foster a reciprocal relationship. This practice emphasizes the interconnectedness of all life and the importance of living in harmony with the natural and spiritual worlds. By recognizing and honoring the presence of these spirits and entities, individuals can deepen their spiritual understanding, foster personal growth, and create a meaningful connection with the divine.

Nature spirits often embody the natural world's vitality and consciousness. They are believed to inhabit various natural features, such as forests, rivers, mountains, and groves. Many cultures have rich mythologies and legends about these spirits, often portraying them as guardians of the natural world who demand respect and reverence. In some traditions, nature spirits are depicted as fairies, elves, or devas, each with unique characteristics and domains. The relationship between humans and nature spirits is often reciprocal; humans may offer gifts, prayers, and rituals to honor these spirits, seeking their favor and protection. In return, nature spirits are believed to bless the land and its inhabitants with fertility, harmony, and prosperity. This relationship underscores the interconnectedness of all life and the importance of living in harmony with the natural world. Indigenous cultures, in particular, maintain a strong connection with nature spirits, incorporating them into their daily lives and spiritual practices.

Elementals are a specific category of nature spirits associated with the classical elements of earth, air, fire, and water. Each elemental is believed to embody the essence and qualities of its respective element. Earth elementals, often called gnomes, are associated with stability, fertility, and material wealth. Air elementals, known as sylphs, are linked to intellect, communication, and freedom. Fire elementals, or salamanders, represent transformation, passion, and energy. Water elementals, called undines or nereids, are connected to emotions, intuition, and healing. Working with elementals involves recognizing and honoring their presence in the natural world and within oneself. Elemental magic and rituals often seek to invoke the qualities of the elements and harmonize their energies. For example, a ritual to summon earth elementals might involve burying crystals or planting seeds to symbolize a desire for stability and growth. Similarly, invoking water elementals might involve rituals near rivers or oceans to seek emotional healing and clarity. The balance and harmony of the elements within and around us are essential for spiritual and physical well-being.

Ancestors play a central role in many spiritual traditions, linking the living and the spiritual realm. Ancestral spirits are believed to offer their descendants guidance, protection, and support. They are often honored through rituals, offerings, and remembrance, acknowledging their contributions and maintaining a connection with the past. Ancestor worship and adoration are particularly prominent in African, Asian, and indigenous cultures, where the continuity of family and community is deeply valued. The practice of ancestor veneration involves creating altars or shrines dedicated to one's ancestors, often featuring photographs, heirlooms, and offerings of food, drink, and incense. These altars serve as focal points for communication and communion with the ancestors. Prayers and rituals may be performed to seek the ancestors' guidance, express gratitude, or request assistance. The belief in the continued presence and influence of the ancestors reinforces the idea of an unbroken lineage and the enduring connection between generations.

Spirit guides, also known as guardian spirits or totem animals, are believed to offer protection, wisdom, and support to individuals on their spiritual journeys. These guides are often seen as benevolent beings who help navigate life's challenges and provide insight into one's path and purpose. Spirit guides can take many forms, including animals, mythological creatures, and ancestral spirits. The concept of spirit guides is found in various spiritual traditions, including shamanism, Native American spirituality, and New Age practices. Connecting with a spirit guide often involves meditation, visualization, and other spiritual practices designed to open one's awareness to the presence and messages of the guide. This relationship is highly personal and unique, with the guide offering tailored guidance and support based on the individual's needs and circumstances. Spirit guides are seen as allies on the spiritual journey, providing wisdom and encouragement and helping to align one's actions with their higher purpose.

In shamanic traditions, the shaman serves as an intermediary between the physical and spiritual realms, often working with various spirits and entities. Shamans undergo rigorous training and initiation to develop their abilities to communicate with spirits and perform healing rituals. They may journey to the spirit world through trance, drumming, or other altered states of consciousness, seeking guidance and assistance from spirit allies. The shaman's role is to restore balance and harmony within individuals and the community by addressing spiritual imbalances and facilitating healing. Many spiritual traditions also recognize the existence of darker or evil spirits, often called demons, jinn, or evil spirits. These entities are believed to cause harm, illness, or misfortune and are usually associated with chaos, negativity, and spiritual corruption. Protective rituals and practices are employed to ward off these negative influences and maintain spiritual purity. This can include talismans, prayers, and rituals designed to banish or neutralize harmful entities.

There is a growing interest in working with spirits and other entities in modern spiritual practices as part of a holistic approach to spirituality and self-development. This includes exploring a variety of spiritual traditions and practices, often blending elements from different cultures and belief systems. For example, individuals might combine practices from shamanism, Wicca, and New Age spirituality to create a personalized spiritual path that resonates with their experiences and beliefs. Working with spirits and entities requires a respectful and mindful approach. It is essential to recognize the autonomy and agency of these beings, treating them with reverence and gratitude. This includes awareness of cultural sensitivities and avoiding appropriation or misrepresenting spiritual practices and beliefs. Building a relationship with spirits and entities is a reciprocal process, requiring time, dedication, and a willingness to listen and learn.

The concept of spirits and entities also extends to the animistic worldview, where all things—living and non-living—are believed to possess a spirit or consciousness. This perspective emphasizes the interconnectedness and sacredness of all life, encouraging a deep respect for nature and the environment. Animism is a foundational belief in many indigenous cultures, where the natural world is seen as alive and imbued with spiritual significance. Animism involves recognizing and honoring the spirits of plants, animals, stones, and other natural features, often through rituals, offerings, and communication. This relationship fosters a deep sense of connection and responsibility towards the natural world, emphasizing the importance of living in harmony with all beings.

The role of spirits and entities in healing practices is also significant. Many traditional healing systems, such as those in African, Native American, and Asian cultures, involve the assistance of spirits and ancestors in diagnosing and treating illness. Healers, shamans, and medicine people often work with spirit allies to identify the spiritual root of physical or emotional ailments and to facilitate healing. This holistic approach recognizes the interconnectedness of mind, body, and spirit and the importance of addressing all aspects of a person's well-being.

In contemporary spiritual practices, there is a growing recognition of the therapeutic benefits of connecting with spirits and entities. Mediumship, channeling, and spirit communication are often used to gain insight, guidance, and healing. These practices involve developing one's intuitive abilities and opening oneself to receive messages and energy from the spiritual realm. The presence of spirit guides and allies can provide comfort, support, and a sense of connection to something greater than oneself.

The ethical considerations of working with spirits and entities are also essential to address. Respect, consent, and integrity are fundamental principles in these practices. It is necessary to approach spirits and entities with humility and gratitude, recognizing their autonomy and agency. Consent involves seeking permission from the spirits before engaging with them and being attentive to their responses and boundaries. Integrity consists in maintaining honesty, transparency, and ethical conduct in all interactions with the spiritual realm.

In conclusion, believing in spirits and other entities encompasses many beings, including nature spirits, elementals, ancestors, and guides. These entities play vital roles in many spiritual traditions, serving as intermediaries between humans and the divine and offering guidance, protection, and wisdom. Working with these spirits involves a combination of rituals, offerings, prayers, and personal practices designed to honor their presence and foster a reciprocal relationship. This practice emphasizes the interconnectedness of all life and the importance of living in harmony with the natural and spiritual worlds. By recognizing and honoring the presence of these spirits and entities, individuals can deepen their spiritual understanding, foster personal growth, and create a meaningful connection with the divine. The animistic worldview, which recognizes the spirit in all things, further emphasizes the sacredness of nature and the importance of living in balance with the environment. The role of spirits and entities in healing practices highlights the holistic nature of well-being, integrating mind, body, and spirit. Finally, ethical considerations ensure that these practices are conducted with respect, consent, and integrity, fostering a positive and respectful relationship with the spiritual realm. Through these practices, individuals can cultivate a profound and transformative relationship with the spirits and entities that inhabit the world around them.

CHAPTER VI

Living a Wiccan Lifestyle

Integrating Wicca into Daily Life

Integrating Wicca into daily life involves more than performing rituals and observing Sabbats; it is about weaving the principles and practices of Wicca into the fabric of everyday living. At its core, Wicca emphasizes the interconnectedness of all life, the reverence for nature, and the honoring of the divine in all its forms. By practicing mindfulness and presence, individuals can transform mundane activities into sacred rituals, fostering a deeper connection with the spiritual world and enhancing their overall well-being.

One of the foundational aspects of Wicca is the recognition of the divine in the natural world. This worldview encourages practitioners to cultivate a deep respect and reverence for nature. Daily mindfulness practices, such as taking a moment to appreciate the beauty of a sunrise or sunset, can help individuals connect with the rhythms of nature. Walking in the park, tending to a garden, or simply sitting under a tree can become acts of devotion, allowing Wiccans to feel the presence of the divine in their surroundings.

Morning routines can be infused with Wiccan spirituality through simple yet meaningful practices. Upon waking, practitioners might start their day with a brief meditation or prayer, setting intentions for the day ahead. This practice helps to center the mind and align it with spiritual goals. Lighting a candle on an altar, saying a few words of gratitude, or drawing a tarot card for guidance can also be powerful ways to begin the day with mindfulness and purpose.

Integrating Wicca into daily life often involves creating sacred spaces within the home. These spaces, such as altars, serve as focal points for meditation, prayer, and ritual. An altar can be a small table adorned with candles, crystals, incense, and the God and Goddess representations. Regularly at the altar, even for a few minutes daily, can help practitioners stay connected to their spiritual practice. This daily ritual fosters a sense of sacredness and presence, transforming the home into a sanctuary of spiritual growth.

Mindfulness in daily activities is a critical component of integrating Wicca into everyday life. Mundane tasks such as cooking, cleaning, and even commuting can be transformed into acts of mindfulness and devotion. For instance, preparing a meal can become a sacred ritual by consciously choosing ingredients, blessing the food, and expressing gratitude for the nourishment it provides. Cleaning the house can clear away stagnant energy and create a harmonious environment. Even a daily commute can be an opportunity for reflection and connection with the divine by listening to spiritual music or reciting mantras.

One of the central tenets of Wicca is the concept of "As Above, So Below," which reflects the belief that the macrocosm of the universe is mirrored in the microcosm of our individual lives. This principle can be applied to daily routines by recognizing that every action has spiritual significance, no matter how small. Practicing mindfulness and presence in these actions helps create a sense of harmony and balance within oneself and in the greater cosmos.

The Wheel of the Year, a central aspect of Wiccan practice, offers a framework for integrating spirituality into daily life. The eight Sabbats, or seasonal festivals, mark the turning points of the natural cycle and provide opportunities for reflection and celebration. By observing these Sabbats and incorporating their themes into daily routines, practitioners can stay attuned to the rhythms of nature and life cycles. For example, during Samhain, a time for honoring ancestors, individuals might set aside time each day to remember loved ones who have passed. During Beltane, a celebration of fertility and new growth, practitioners might spend more time outdoors, planting seeds or connecting with the earth.

Incorporating elements of ritual into daily life can also enhance mindfulness and presence. Rituals need not elaborate to be effective; simple acts can carry profound meaning. Lighting a candle, burning incense, or praying before meals are all examples of daily rituals that help individuals stay connected to their spiritual practice. The key is to perform these actions with intention and awareness, recognizing them as opportunities to honor the divine and cultivate a sense of sacredness in everyday life.

Meditation is another powerful tool for integrating Wicca into daily routines. Regular meditation helps quiet the mind, increase awareness, and deepen one's connection to the spiritual realm. Many forms of meditation can be incorporated into a Wiccan practice, including guided meditations, breathwork, and visualization. For example, a practitioner might meditate on the moon's phases, visualizing its energy and contemplating its influence on their life. This practice can attune individuals to the lunar cycles and enhance their understanding of the interconnectedness of all things.

In addition to meditation, mindfulness techniques such as grounding and centering can be incorporated into daily life. Grounding involves connecting with the earth's energy, which can be achieved through walking barefoot on the grass, hugging a tree, or visualizing roots extending from one's body into the ground. Centering involves bringing one's focus inward and finding balance and calm. These practices can be beneficial during stress or when feeling disconnected from one's spiritual path.

Another important aspect of Wiccan practice is the use of tools and symbols. These tools, such as athames, chalices, and pentacles, are tangible representations of spiritual concepts and can be integrated into daily life. For example, wearing a pentacle pendant or carrying a small crystal can remind one of one's spiritual beliefs and intentions. Using these tools in daily rituals and routines helps to create a sense of continuity and connection with the spiritual realm.

The practice of divination is also an integral part of Wicca and can be incorporated into daily life. Divination tools such as tarot cards, runes, and scrying mirrors provide insight and guidance, helping practitioners to navigate their spiritual journeys. Setting aside time each day to draw a card or cast a rune can become a meaningful ritual, offering opportunities for reflection and self-discovery. These practices help to cultivate intuition and enhance one's connection with the divine.

Gratitude is a fundamental aspect of Wiccan spirituality and can be cultivated through daily mindfulness practices. Taking time each day to express gratitude for the blessings in one's life helps to shift focus away from negativity and fosters a positive outlook. This can be done through journaling, prayer, or simply taking a moment to acknowledge the things one is thankful for silently. Practicing gratitude enhances one's sense of connection to the divine and reinforces the belief in the abundance and generosity of the universe.

Connecting with the natural elements is another way to integrate Wicca into daily life. The elements of earth, air, fire, and water are seen as the universe's building blocks and are honored in many Wiccan rituals. Practitioners can incorporate the elements into their daily routines by working with them directly. For example, taking a walk in nature (earth), practicing deep breathing exercises (air), lighting a candle (fire), or spending time near a body of water (water) are all ways to connect with the elements and honor their presence in one's life.

Incorporating the moon's cycles into daily life is another way to align with Wiccan principles. The moon's phases influence the natural world and human experience. Practitioners can attune to these cycles by observing the moon's phases and performing rituals or meditations corresponding to its energy. For example, the new moon is a time for setting intentions and new beginnings, while the full moon is a time for manifestation and completion. By aligning daily practices with the lunar cycles, individuals can deepen their connection to the rhythms of nature and enhance their spiritual growth.

The practice of magick is also central to Wicca and can be integrated into daily life through tiny, intentional acts. Magick is the art of influencing reality through focused intention and energy. Practitioners can incorporate magick into their routines by performing simple spells, such as lighting a candle with a specific purpose, creating herbal sachets for protection or healing, or reciting affirmations. These magick acts help empower individuals, align their intentions with their actions, and manifest their desires in the physical world.

In addition to these practices, community, and connection with other practitioners play a significant role in integrating Wicca into daily life. Engaging with a coven, attending public rituals, or participating in online communities can provide support, inspiration, and a sense of belonging. Sharing experiences, learning from others, and participating in group rituals can deepen one's understanding of Wicca and enhance community and interconnectedness.

Balancing the spiritual with the mundane is crucial to integrating Wicca into daily life. While spiritual practices and rituals are essential, attending to the practical aspects of life is equally important. Wicca teaches that the sacred and the mundane are interconnected, and by approaching everyday tasks with mindfulness and presence, individuals can create a harmonious balance. This holistic approach encourages practitioners to find meaning and purpose in all aspects of life, recognizing that every moment offers an opportunity for spiritual growth and connection.

In conclusion, integrating Wicca into daily life involves weaving its principles and practices into everyday living. By practicing mindfulness and presence, individuals can transform mundane activities into sacred rituals, fostering a deeper connection with the spiritual world. From morning routines and creating sacred spaces to practicing gratitude and connecting with nature, many ways exist to incorporate Wiccan spirituality into daily life. Meditation, mindfulness techniques, tools and symbols, divination, and magick all offer opportunities for reflection, self-discovery, and manifestation. Community and connection with other practitioners provide support and inspiration while balancing the spiritual with the mundane encourages a holistic approach to life. By integrating Wicca into daily routines and rituals, individuals can cultivate a profound and transformative connection with the divine, enhancing their overall well-being and spiritual growth.

Wiccan Ethics and Morality

Wicca, a modern pagan religion, strongly emphasizes ethics and morality. At its core, Wiccan ethics revolve around the Wiccan Rede, a guiding principle that succinctly captures the essence of Wiccan moral philosophy: "An it harm none, do what ye will." This maxim, while simple in its wording, embodies a complex and profound ethical framework that emphasizes personal responsibility, respect for others, and a deep reverence for nature. In addition to the Wiccan Rede, environmental stewardship and sustainability are central to Wiccan practice, reflecting the religion's deep connection to the natural world and the belief in the sacredness of all life.

The Wiccan Rede is the foundational ethical principle for Wiccans, guiding their actions and decisions. The phrase "An it harms none" emphasizes avoiding harm to oneself, others, and the environment. This principle encourages Wiccans to consider their actions' potential consequences and strive for actions that are beneficial or at least neutral in their impact. It calls for a high degree of personal responsibility, requiring individuals to be mindful of how their actions affect the world around them.

Interpreting the Wiccan Rede requires careful consideration and discernment. "Harm" can be understood in various ways, including physical, emotional, and spiritual harm. For example, actions that cause bodily injury, emotional distress, or spiritual imbalance would be considered harmful and, therefore, contrary to the Rede. This broad understanding of harm encourages Wiccans to develop empathy and compassion, fostering a sense of interconnectedness and mutual respect.

The second part of the Rede, "Do what ye will," emphasizes personal freedom and autonomy. It suggests that individuals pursue their paths and make their own choices, provided they do not cause harm. This aspect of the Rede empowers Wiccans to explore their spirituality and personal growth in meaningful ways. It acknowledges the diversity of human experience and the importance of individual expression.

Balancing personal freedom with the responsibility to avoid harm is a central challenge in Wiccan ethics. This balance requires ongoing reflection and self-awareness. Wiccans are encouraged to evaluate their actions and intentions regularly, considering whether they align with the Rede. This reflective practice helps to cultivate a sense of integrity and accountability, fostering ethical behavior and personal growth.

In addition to the Wiccan Rede, the Law of Threefold Return is another crucial ethical concept in Wicca. This law posits that whatever energy a person puts out into the world, whether positive or negative, will be returned to them threefold. This belief reinforces the importance of ethical behavior, encouraging Wiccans to act with kindness, generosity, and integrity. The Law of Threefold Return serves as a reminder that actions have consequences and that living ethically can lead to positive outcomes and personal fulfillment.

Environmental stewardship is a core aspect of Wiccan ethics, reflecting the religion's deep connection to nature. Wiccans believe that the Earth is sacred and that all living beings are interconnected. This belief fosters a sense of reverence and responsibility towards the natural world. Wiccans are encouraged to live in harmony with nature, to protect and preserve the environment, and to promote sustainability.

Practicing environmental stewardship involves adopting sustainable practices in daily life. This can include reducing waste, conserving energy, and using natural resources responsibly. For example, Wiccans might recycle, compost, and use environmentally friendly products. They may also strive to reduce their carbon footprint by using public transportation, carpooling, or biking instead of driving. These actions reflect a commitment to living in harmony with the Earth and minimizing environmental harm.

Many Wiccans also engage in environmental activism, advocating for policies and practices that protect the natural world. This can involve participating in conservation efforts, supporting renewable energy initiatives, and raising awareness about environmental issues. By taking an active role in environmental stewardship, Wiccans demonstrate their commitment to the well-being of the planet and future generations.

Rituals and ceremonies in Wicca often incorporate elements of nature, further emphasizing the religion's connection to the environment. For example, rituals might be held outdoors in natural settings, such as forests, gardens, or near bodies of water. These settings are chosen for their beauty and ability to inspire awe and reverence for the natural world. Rituals may also involve using natural objects, such as stones, plants, and water, as symbols of the elements and the Earth. By incorporating nature into their spiritual practice, Wiccans reinforce their connection to the environment and their commitment to its protection.

The concept of balance is central to Wiccan ethics and environmental stewardship. Wiccans believe in maintaining balance within oneself, in one's relationships, and in the natural world. This belief is reflected in the Wiccan practice of celebrating the cycles of the moon and the seasons. These cycles represent the natural rhythms of life and the interconnectedness of all things. By attuning to these cycles and honoring them through rituals and observances, Wiccans strive to maintain harmony and balance in their lives.

Practicing mindfulness is another crucial aspect of Wiccan ethics and environmental stewardship. Mindfulness involves being fully present in the moment and aware of one's thoughts, feelings, and actions. It encourages individuals to observe their impact on the world and to make conscious choices that align with their values. For example, a mindful approach to consumption might involve considering the environmental impact of a product before purchasing it, choosing to support local and sustainable businesses, and being conscious of waste and resource use. Wiccans can cultivate a deeper awareness of their connection to the Earth and their role in its stewardship by practicing mindfulness.

Wiccan ethics also emphasize the importance of community and collaboration. Wiccans often gather in groups, known as covens, to practice their spirituality and support one another. These communities provide a space for sharing knowledge, resources, and support, fostering a sense of interconnectedness and mutual aid. In the context of environmental stewardship, Wiccan communities can work together on conservation projects, advocacy efforts, and sustainable living initiatives. By collaborating with others, Wiccans can amplify their impact and contribute to the collective well-being of the planet.

Education and awareness are also critical components of Wiccan ethics and environmental stewardship. Wiccans are encouraged to continually learn about the natural world, environmental issues, and sustainable practices. This knowledge can inform their actions and help them make informed choices that align with their values. Sharing this knowledge through teaching, writing, or advocacy can raise awareness and inspire positive change. Wiccans can contribute to a more sustainable and harmonious world by promoting education and awareness.

In addition to environmental stewardship, Wiccan ethics encompass a broader commitment to social justice and equality. Wiccans believe in all beings' inherent worth and dignity and strive to promote fairness and equality in their interactions. The Wiccan principles of respect, compassion, and empathy reflect this commitment to social justice. Wiccans are encouraged to stand against discrimination, oppression, and injustice and to work towards a more inclusive and equitable society. This commitment to social justice aligns with the broader ethical framework of Wicca, which emphasizes the interconnectedness of all life and the importance of living in harmony with others.

Ethical principles also guide the practice of magick in Wicca. Magick is seen as a tool for personal and spiritual growth, and the Wiccan Rede and the Law of Threefold Return govern its practice. Wiccans are encouraged to use magick responsibly and with intention, always considering the potential impact of their actions. This ethical approach to magick emphasizes the importance of using one's power for positive purposes and aligning with one's values. It also reinforces the belief in personal responsibility and the interconnectedness of all actions.

In conclusion, Wiccan ethics and morality are deeply rooted in the principles of the Wiccan Rede, environmental stewardship, and social justice. The Wiccan Rede, which emphasizes avoiding harm and promoting personal freedom, is a foundational guide for ethical behavior. It encourages Wiccans to live with integrity, compassion, and responsibility, fostering a sense of interconnectedness and mutual respect. Environmental stewardship is a central aspect of Wiccan ethics, reflecting the religion's deep connection to nature and the belief in the sacredness of all life. Practicing sustainability, mindfulness, and activism, Wiccans strive to protect and preserve the environment, recognizing their responsibility to future generations. The ethical practice of magick, guided by the Wiccan Rede and the Law of Threefold Return, emphasizes the importance of intention and commitment. Wiccans work towards a more sustainable, harmonious, and just world through education, awareness, and community collaboration. By integrating these ethical principles into their daily lives, Wiccans can cultivate a profound and transformative connection with the divine, the natural world, and their fellow beings.

Building a Wiccan Community

Building a Wiccan community involves creating a network of individuals who share similar spiritual beliefs and practices. This process includes finding and participating in local and online groups and hosting gatherings and rituals that foster connection, support, and growth. A thriving Wiccan community provides a sense of belonging and enhances spiritual practice through shared experiences, knowledge, and energy. By actively engaging in community-building activities, Wiccans can create spaces where mutual respect, learning, and spiritual development flourish.

Finding local Wiccan groups can be a rewarding experience that begins with research and outreach. Many Wiccan communities are informal and can be discovered through word of mouth, local metaphysical shops, or community bulletin boards. These physical spaces often serve as hubs for Wiccans and other pagans, providing resources such as books, ritual tools, and information about local events. Attending workshops, lectures, and open rituals hosted by these shops can be an excellent way to meet like-minded individuals and learn about local groups.

Online resources have become invaluable for finding Wiccan communities, especially for those who live in areas with fewer local options. Social media platforms, forums, and websites dedicated to Wicca and paganism offer opportunities to connect with others. Websites like Meetup, Witchvox, and Facebook groups allow Wiccans to search for local or virtual gatherings and discussions. Engaging in online communities can provide connection and support, offering a space to share experiences, ask questions, and learn from others. These platforms often host virtual rituals, discussions, and workshops, making it possible to participate in communal activities from anywhere in the world.

Participating in local and online Wiccan groups involves active engagement and respectful interaction. In local groups, attending regular meetings, rituals, and social events helps build relationships and trust within the community. Participation might include contributing to discussions, sharing personal experiences, and assisting in organizing events. Respect for group norms and practices is crucial, as each community may have its traditions and expectations. For online groups, participation can involve posting on forums, joining virtual meetings, and contributing to discussions. Online etiquette, such as being respectful and considerate in interactions, is essential for maintaining a positive and supportive community atmosphere.

Hosting gatherings and rituals is a significant aspect of building a Wiccan community. These events provide opportunities for communal worship, celebration, and spiritual growth. Hosting can range from small, informal gatherings to larger, structured rituals. It requires planning, organization, and a deep understanding of Wiccan practices and principles.

The first step in hosting a Wiccan gathering is choosing an appropriate space. This could be a private home, a public park, or a rented venue. The space should be conducive to ritual work, offering privacy, a connection to nature, and enough room for participants to move comfortably. If the event is outdoors, considerations such as weather, accessibility, and local regulations are essential. Indoor spaces should be free from distractions and provide a sense of sacredness and tranquility.

Creating a welcoming and inclusive environment is crucial for successful gatherings. This involves setting a positive and respectful tone and ensuring all participants feel comfortable and valued. Clear communication about the event's purpose, schedule, and any requirements (such as items to bring or attire) helps participants prepare and feel at ease. Inclusivity also means being mindful of different experience levels and accommodating various needs and preferences.

The structure of a Wiccan ritual often follows a traditional format, which includes elements such as casting a circle, calling the quarters, invoking deities, conducting the leading working or celebration, sharing food and drink (cakes and ale), and closing the circle. Each element serves a specific purpose and contributes to the ritual's energy and focus. Careful planning and preparation are essential to ensure that the ritual flows smoothly and that all necessary materials and tools are available.

Casting the circle is a fundamental part of Wiccan rituals. It creates a sacred space that separates the mundane from the spiritual, providing a safe and focused environment for the ritual. The circle is typically cast using tools such as an athame, wand, or staff, and it can be visualized as a sphere of protective energy. Calling the quarters involves invoking the elemental energies of earth, air, fire, and water, often represented by the cardinal directions (north, east, south, and west). This practice helps to balance and harmonize the ritual space, drawing on the strengths and qualities of each element.

Invoking deities or spiritual entities is another crucial aspect of Wiccan rituals. This can involve calling upon the God and Goddess, specific deities from various pantheons, or other spiritual beings relevant to the ritual's purpose. The invocation is typically done through spoken words, chants, or songs, and it invites the presence and guidance of these divine forces. The leading working of the ritual can vary widely, depending on its purpose. It might include spellwork, meditations, blessings, seasonal celebrations, or other magical and spiritual practice forms.

Sharing food and drink, often called cakes and ale, is a communal and celebratory part of Wiccan rituals. This practice symbolizes the sharing of blessings and gratitude for the earth's abundance. The food and drink are blessed and passed around the circle, fostering community and connection among participants. Closing the circle involves thanking the deities and elemental energies, releasing the sacred space, and grounding any excess energy. This helps bring participants back to their everyday awareness and concludes the ritual respectfully and balanced.

Hosting gatherings and rituals also involves practical considerations, such as ensuring the safety and comfort of participants. This includes providing adequate lighting, seating, and facilities and being prepared for emergencies. Clear guidelines and expectations regarding behavior, participation, and respect for the ritual space help to create a positive and harmonious environment.

Building a Wiccan community through hosting gatherings and rituals can profoundly impact participants. These events provide opportunities for shared spiritual experiences, personal growth, and mutual support. They foster a sense of belonging and connection, reinforcing the values and principles of Wicca. By creating communal worship and celebration spaces, Wiccans can strengthen their spiritual practice and build lasting relationships within the community.

In addition to physical gatherings, online rituals, and events have become increasingly popular and accessible. Virtual platforms allow Wiccans from different locations to come together, share experiences, and participate in rituals. Hosting online events involves similar planning and organization as in-person gatherings, with additional considerations for technology and accessibility. Clear communication, inclusivity, and respect remain essential, ensuring all participants feel welcome and engaged.

Building a Wiccan community also involves ongoing efforts to nurture and sustain relationships. This can include regular communication, such as newsletters, social media updates, and email lists, to keep members informed and connected. Organizing social events, study groups, and collaborative projects can further strengthen the community and provide diverse opportunities for engagement. Supporting one another through life's challenges and celebrations fosters a sense of solidarity and mutual care, reinforcing the bonds within the community.

Mentorship and leadership play essential roles in building and sustaining a Wiccan community. Experienced practitioners can offer guidance, support, and education to newcomers, helping them to develop their practice and integrate into the community. Leadership involves facilitating events, organizing activities, and ensuring the community aligns with Wiccan values and principles. Effective leadership is collaborative, inclusive, and responsive to the needs and aspirations of the community.

Education and shared learning are central to the growth and development of a Wiccan community. Offering classes, workshops, and discussion groups on various aspects of Wicca and related topics can enhance the knowledge and skills of community members. These educational opportunities provide a space for exploration, questioning, and deepening understanding. Sharing resources, such as books, articles, and online content, can further support the ongoing learning and development of the community.

Inclusivity and diversity are essential values in building a Wiccan community. Wicca is a diverse and eclectic spiritual path, and communities can benefit from embracing different perspectives, traditions, and experiences. This inclusivity enriches the community, fostering creativity, learning, and mutual respect. Ensuring that all members feel valued and heard, regardless of their background or experience, helps create a welcoming and supportive environment.

CONCLUSION

At the end of "The Essence of Wiccan Living and Lifestyle: Crafting a Magical Life," we hope that this exploration of Wicca's practice has shed light on its significant influence on day-to-day existence. Wicca is a spiritual tapestry woven with strands of ancient knowledge, reverence for nature, and a deep connection to the divine in all its manifestations. By exploring its rich traditions, ethical foundations, and magical practices, you've launched on a personal and spiritual growth journey.

Thanks to this book, You have become familiar with the rhythms of the Wiccan Wheel of the Year, which honors the Sabbats and Esbats that signal the passing of time. You now know about the gods, implements, and symbols that enhance Wiccan ceremonies and the transformative and empowering magical techniques. Harmonizing with nature, respecting life's cycles, and creating a life filled with meaning and holiness are the cornerstones of Wiccan living.

By embracing Wiccan values, you open the door to a well-balanced, meaningful, and deeply connected life. Wicca offers a path to happiness and enlightenment through rituals, spell casting, or simply appreciating the beauty of the natural world. As you continue your Wiccan path, may you find insight, inspiration, and a strong sense of community within our magical tradition.

I am deeply grateful for your commitment to exploring the core principles of a Wiccan existence. May your path be blessed with love, light, and the enduring enchantment of the Wiccan way as you continue your journey.